DEDICATION:

I have been blessed with the honor of helping families grow to be more creative and caring. Over the years, many have told me at the end of a family therapy session, "This is a lot to remember, you should write a book!"

So, I dedicate this book to the patients who asked, no, demanded, that I write it.

Special thanks goes to Geri, an amazing person who warms the hearts of all who know her and the only one I know who can put up with me.

Thank you for encouraging my behavior.

Philip Copitch, Ph.D.
2004

I0430166

Contents

Life's Laws For New Adults

An inside look at how to deal with the real world.

An authoritative guide to winning at the unforgiving game of life.

Mastering Your Social I.Q.

Philip Copitch, Ph.D.
Cognitive Behavioral Therapist

PARENTAL WARNING:

Rated
R
Restricted

This book is rated "R" due to content matter and language. It is not intended for children or young / immature teens.
Do not read this book if you are offended by obscenity, difficult life issues, or the sarcastic truth.

HERE TO SERVE YOU:

Hutzpah Press titles are available in quantity discounts for promotions, premiums and fund raisers.

**Our titles can be custom imprinted
with your name and information.**

FOR FURTHER INFORMATION PLEASE CONTACT:

HUTZPAH PRESS
POX 400 IGO CA 96047
PHONE: (530) 244-7528
E-MAIL: DrPhil@CopitchInc.com
www.CopitchInc.com

CEUs available for therapists at:
CEUforTherapists.com

INTRODUCTION

Please be advised that this book is serious. It is not a self help book designed to simply make you feel good. It will not show you how to blame others. It sells no crystals, food supplements, pills, or prayers. It is an in-your-face, mega dose of reality. This book is about how to get what you want, and avoid what you don't want in your life. This book is the straight dope on how to deal with friends, family, teachers, jerks, employers, authority figures, and yourself.

For that reason, I have decided not to soft soap any part of it. This book is definitely not for everybody. Many parents will not want their teenagers to read this. Many adults will wish that they had read this book years ago (probably when they were older teenagers).

SOME SERIOUS WARNINGS:

This book is intended for maturing young adults fifteen to ninety-nine years of age.

If you are offended by words that are considered by many adults to be obscene or profane—do not read past this introduction. In this introduction there is no harsh language or real life drama. This introduction is rated G.

This book contains words that would get you kicked out of most schools if you spoke them in class. But, none that are not known by 99.99 percent of kids by the seventh grade. If this book were a movie, it would most definitely be rated R! I expect that this book will be banned by uptight bigoted groups that are worried that its contents will soil the lily white brains of their *impressionable* children.

WHY SHOULD YOU BOTHER
TO READ THIS BOOK?

I have been a therapist for over twenty years. In that time I have worked with lots of people of all ages. I have seen a lot of bad stuff. However, I have also seen some wondrous things that give one hope that mankind has a small chance of still being here in a thousand years.

I truly believe that, with information, most people will make the correct choices for themselves. But, with limited information, most people are destined to relive the same disaster, over and over. Same story, different players.

I'm not a born again anything. I was born a skeptic and I expect to die a skeptic. I also expect a lot out of myself, and you. I expect us both to follow our moral beliefs. I expect us both to question authority. I expect us both to question and challenge our own thoughts. I want us both to be kind to ourselves and to others. However, I think all this is hard to do because we share this planet with some real jerks (I cleaned the last statement up a lot!).

Over the years I have learned a lot from the people I have had the honor to counsel. I have noticed that people who do well in life possess certain skills, and people without these same skills tend to screw up. These skills are not taught in school. In fact, teachers, like most adults, tend not to possess them. People with this "secret" knowledge avoid what they don't want and find what they do.

That's what this book is all about. To follow are the ten gifts that I would like you to have to help you get the most out of your short time on this planet. Life is very short. It is limited to less than 100 years. One hundred sounds like a lot, but I have lost a few friends in their twenties and scores of friends in their fifties and sixties. And sadly, I have helped many families through the loss of their young child or bright eyed teenager. Trust me, life is short and too easily squandered.

You have to run your life—not just "be" alive. This book focuses on how to run your life; how to take an active role in your existence on this planet.

Last warning: Don't write me and complain that this book is vulgar or not politically correct. I know all that—I wrote it! You have been thoroughly forewarned. By turning this page you are willing to take stock in yourself and look into how you can take realistic control of your world.

Welcome to the real world, the world most people never quite understand!

—>>>>>>>>>>

PARENTAL WARNING:	
Rated **R** Restricted	This book is rated "R" due to content matter and language. It is not intended for children or young / immature teens.

Do not read this book if you are offended by obscenity, difficult life issues, or the sarcastic truth.

Life's Law #1

There are rules—deal with it or lose

1. LIFE'S LAW #1

There are rules—deal with it or lose

Most people, no matter their age, refuse to accept this rule. I hear it all the time, "I shouldn't have to ..." or, "It's not fair ..." To which I say, "Deal with it or lose!"

The fact is that life is a game. Like any game, life has rules. Unlike most games, the game of life has <u>hidden</u> rules. You need to get your head around this fact, or life will eat you alive.

What Law #1 teaches us is that every situation you encounter has rules. They happen with or without your knowledge. Without your approval. And either way, life's rules influence you everyday.

When you walk into Mr. Monotone's fifth period history class there are rules that you need to deal with. No one asked if you wanted to play by these rules, you're just stuck with them. You are just expected to follow them. In addition, all situations have socially "known rules" and "secret rules" that must be figured out.

It is your responsibility to figure out the rules for any given situation and use this information to your best interest. That's right. The reason you need to figure out the rules is so that you can get <u>your</u> needs met. Get what you want and avoid what you don't want so you can win at this game called life!

I want you to notice that I am not embarrassed by this level of selfishness. In fact, I pity the dumb asses that don't figure out what is going on and constantly bash their thick heads against life's walls. It is your responsibility, to yourself, to learn how to deal with your world.

Socially known rules, such as the classroom rules in Mr. Monotone's class, are usually easy to find. Mr. Monotone probably droned on and on the very first day, boring you to death about his "classroom rules." My assumption is that by now you know the basic classroom rules and Mr. Monotone is as informative as the flight attendant who stands in the front of the cabin and instructs you on how to put on or take off a seat belt. What's with that? I would think that 99.99% of the airline passengers drove to the airport. Didn't they use their seat belts? I guess that the airlines believe that if you're willing to pay hundreds of dollars to cram your ass into a narrow airline seat, you're probably not smart enough to understand the mechanical physics of a common seat belt.

Law #1 is about the "secret rules" of dealing with Mr. Monotone. You need to know about these secret rules to navigate Mr. Monotone's class. It is important that you figure out how to deal with

I worked with a caring educator who wanted all the students in his school to learn critical thinking skills as well as nuggets of facts that they could place correctly on the S.A.T. answer sheet.

On numerous occasions he proposed to the school board that he wanted to start a teacher evaluation program. He explained that many universities used questionnaires to judge the teaching staff from the student point of view.

Every year his project was turned down. The two biggest reasons were, "The teachers will feel pressured by the students' power" and "The students would use it as a personality contest."

Unfortunately, to date the program has not been implemented.

Mr. Monotone and use this knowledge to get your needs met.

Let's look at how this might work. During the first half hour of the first class you check out the lay of the land. You realize that even though Mr. Monotone said, "If you have any questions you must raise your hand." He left out the secret rule that reads: "I'm really tired of you smart ass kids. After twenty-two years of teaching I have figured out what I need to teach, and if you simply pay attention I'll tell you what I expect you to regurgitate on your test." How the hell did you figure out this secret rule? You watched. When Betty Brownnose, sitting up front all perky like, asked a question, Mr. Monotone sarcastically let her know that he thought he clearly covered that already. He made it clear to all who were watching that his words said "ask questions" but he didn't really want to be bothered with answering them.

Is this fair? Absolutely not. Is it something you need to deal with? Hell yeah! This teaching drone holds your grade in his left hand. If he squeezes, your voice changes. When the principal comes by, you wouldn't be surprised if Mr. Monotone perked up and became Mr. Stereo. He knows the secret rules that he learned from watching principals. He probably learned to leave his classroom rules out so that the principal could "accidentally" spy them. He learned it's a good idea to have a clear rule that encourages one's students to ask questions. He learned that as long as he gives lip service to the principal, the principal won't care that Mr. Monotone is actually discouraging questions in the privacy of his classroom domain. Adults live in the same world teens live in. Smart adults know that Law #1 is powerful.

ALL THINGS BEING EQUAL,
TRUST BEHAVIOR

Many years ago my oldest child, who was about three years old, was baking cookies with his mother, Geri. This may not sound all that remarkable, but it was. In the world of Norman Rockwell paintings moms bake cookies with their children. But, not in the Copitch household. Let me explain. Geri thinks I'm fat. She is very nice about it, she doesn't tease me or make faces, but she believes that I am fat. I will go so far as to say that it is one of her missions in life to un-fat me. I'm pretty sure that she believes that sugar is the devil's dandruff and that it is her job to keep sugar out of the house. Or, more specifically, out of me. So, making cookies at the Copitch household takes an act of Congress.

On this day, mom and son were baking cookies. Somehow, little Ethan had enough charm that Mom announced during the cookie making process, "Let's make a really big cookie for Daddy." Ethan was excited, while I was watching closely, trying to figure out how he had manipulated his mother so well for my benefit (I am not opposed to learning from a three year old if it gets me a big ass cookie).

A half hour later, when I entered the kitchen, Ethan was very happy to show me the cookie "he" had made me. Ethan also informed me, "You no want, Ethy's cookie!" To which Mom interjected, "No Ethy, that's Daddy's cookie, it is not for you." He seemed to take this in stride. I assumed he'd already had this conversation with his mother.

By chance, a little while later I walked out of the den into the living room. Ethan stopped short and quickly put something behind his back. He looked up at me with fear in his eyes. He had cookie crumbs all around his mouth and lots more on the chest of his footed, terry cloth, blue pajamas.

"Ethan" I asked, "Are you eating Daddy's cookie?" I didn't have to be much of a detective. The little fellow was so tiny that I could see "Daddy's cookie" peeking from behind him on both sides.

"No ... I no eat Daddy cookie." His eyes gave nothing away. He then looked at his own pale blue terry covered little feet. There were lots more crumbs there too. He tried to brush them off. First, with his right toes, then with his left toes. He took a quick look up at me. I assumed my face was red because I was trying not to bust a gut and laugh at him. This was one damn cute kid. He then proceeded to bend deeply to brush off the crumbs with his hand. His other hand was holding the "big" cookie behind his back, now in my full view. His little hand was covered with cookie crumbs, so no matter how hard he tried, he was adding more crumbs to his feet than he was brushing off.

In a firm but gentle voice I asked, "Ethan is there something you need to tell me?"

At this he stood up straight, handed me my cookie and calmly stated, "I brought you your cookie Daddy," then scampered off upstairs. Thinking about it as I write this, I don't think I ever busted him for stealing my cookie.

So, why did I tell you this story? To show you that behavior counts. Words are of limited importance.

In the real world—behavior counts. If your friend says that he is going to quit smoking for the hundredth time this year, you wouldn't be too impressed. But, smoke-free for six days, that counts. If this same friend says, "At the end of this pack I'm quitting," it's hard to believe him. His behavior says, "I smoke." His words sound like what they are—a lie. Harsh but true, deal with it.

Often the secret rules are first seen as behaviors. It is your job to figure out the unspoken rules so that others can't use your lack of knowledge against you. If you are sure that Mr. Monotone is burned out and useless as a teacher, it doesn't change the fact that he is giving you your grade. It is your job to figure out what you need to do so you can get him to give you the grade you want. Please note, I didn't say the grade your mom wants you to get. I clearly stated "the grade you want." So, if you want a D+ figure out what you need to do to get it. If you want an A+ figure out what you need to do to get it. Once you have figured it out, then you need to ask yourself if it's worth it to you. If it is, go for it.

Most teens get pissed that their teachers are not acting honestly. The fact is, no one who counts, such as the principal, could give a rat's ass about your opinion. That is, except for you. You count, but you don't have any power in this situation. So, you need to figure out what the unspoken rules are and use them to your best advantage. This is cold but true, deal with it.

You need to keep focused on what you need from this class. Usually, it is to learn something and to get a good grade. So, stay focused on this, learn stuff, and get a good grade. Figure out the rules and use them to your benefit.

Some of you are probably thinking, "I don't want to figure out the rules, it's all bogus anyway, get off my ass!" To this I soundly say, "Bullshit!"

I don't believe for one second that you are willing to miss an

People confuse freedom with license.

opportunity to get something you want. That's counter intuitive. People don't work like that . We all want. It's built into our DNA. We are basically a bag of mostly water that wants stuff. We want food, water, to be liked, to have sex, own a car, and not to be bitched at. We all want.

People set up attitudes to deflect pain. "I'd rather wipe shit on others before they wipe shit on me." That's like banging your head on a brick wall so when you stop, it feels good. That's completely stupid. The world is not impressed with your attitude. In fact, if your attitude is too hard to deal with, most adults will work against you just because they can. If your behavior's so crappy or scary that others are afraid of you, our society will lock your ass up. In the year 2000, the Justice Department reported that 6.47 million adults were in jail, on parole, or on probation. That is to say, 1 in every 32 adults in America is being "parented" by the government. Adults tend to get pissed when I refer to jail as parenting. But it is. If you're an adult who is such a screw-up that you can't control yourself, society will send you to your room—Cell J, Tier 112, Attica State Prison. Jail is the adult version of room restrictions. And, probation or parole is the adult version of being grounded. Wow, what a kick in the head. 6.47 million adults can't figure out this game called life either!

In the year 2000, 3.1% of the US adult population was in prison, compared with 1% in 1980.

U.S. Justice Department

You can put a nail into a wall with a rock. But, if you have a hammer only a moron keeps using the rock. Most of us would use the hammer because it works better. If you use life's rules, life works better. However, if you're that moron, stop reading this book. You know everything. You have it all figured out. Stop reading this book! Please donate it to your local public library.

This book is full of tools to make your life path easier. It's your path, you get to do it your way. You can reinvent everything yourself as you travel, or you can pick up some insight from this little book and save yourself a shit load of heartache.

There are rules—deal with it or lose.

Let's look at Life's Law #1 in the real world. The following story shows how some people screw with us just because they can.

MAYO MAYHEM

For years I have gone to an all night poker game with friends the night before Super Bowl Sunday. The game tends to start at about eight. The biggest part of the whole ordeal is the bragging rights that go along with winning. If you win you are hated by your friends all through the Super Bowl game and party. The losers are relentless. "You ripped me a new one last night." "You're such a lucky bastard." "We're not inviting you next year, you dick!" It's great when your oldest friends bitch at you because you kicked their sorry asses again!

Well, to say the least, I was all excited about getting to the card game. Due to things outside of my control we were held up for hours before we could leave. Nothing I could do about it. I was going to be late for the game. Maybe I could get there by 11 o'clock. What a bummer, all those hands that I was planning to win. When we finally got off the highway, the kids were asleep in the back seat. I told my wife that I was going to pop into the grocery store just down the street from the poker game. It was one of those really big grocery store chains that has everything but service. It was five 'til eleven. They close at eleven.

I whizzed down the pet supply aisle and grabbed a five pound bag of dog food. Enough for one meal for my big dog who was traveling in the way back of the wagon. I figured I would get more supplies tomorrow. But I was already late for some serious card playing. I swooped up to the Express Register and plopped my bag on the counter. I handed the clerk a ten.

He put up his hand and said, "Ya have ta use your ATM card."

Not understanding I asked, "What?"

"Ya have ta use your ATM card."

"How come?" I asked as I tried to hand him a perfectly good ten dollar bill.

"Ya have ta use your ATM card cuz I Z-ed out my register."

He gestured to the ATM box. I felt myself getting pissed.

"How come I can't use cash. What grocery store doesn't take cash?"

"Look mister, you can't use cash. I Z-ed out my register already. We close in just a few minutes. Do ya want the dog food or not?"

By this time a small line was behind me.

I took a few seconds to gather information. I analyzed the

Parents are sometimes a bit of a disappointment to their children. They don't fulfil the promise of their early years.

Anthony Powell
A Buyers Market

scene, I compiled the secret rules and I gave myself permission to lie. "I'm sorry dude, but the guy on aisle 5 told me I had to pay for the mayonnaise I broke. All I have is cash."

The cashier rolled his eyes and poked away at the keys of the machine. He turned a key and pressed in some more numbers. The bell went off and the cash drawer popped open. As he was closing the drawer he looked at me and asked, "What kind of mayo did you bust?"

Calmly I said, "I didn't break any mayo. I just want the dog food." I offered up the same ten again.

He snatched the bill from my hand, grunted a few times and pushed the change back into my hand.

I picked up the bag of dog food and headed for the exit. Standing at the exit was an older man with a white apron stained with blood. The butcher I guess. The butcher was starting to laugh, something about "...You got him" as I headed out the door. As I got to the car, my son Ethan, then about ten, was rubbing sleep out of his eyes.

"Daddy," he said as I opened the car door. "There's a fight."

As I drove out of the parking lot, I saw the cashier and the butcher rolling around, arms flailing, in the doorway of the store. The automatic doors were trying, unsuccessfully, to close on them.

So what does this have to do with Life's Law #1? I was just trying to buy dog food and the cashier was making it hard for me. I'm sure the owner of the Super Store wanted the cashier to take my cash. In fact, I'm sure that they want to take all my cash. But, the cashier had his own "secret rules." My guess is that he wanted to get off as soon as the store closed. He probably

> *I always tried to make it a habit to do things good.*
>
> Sandra Day O'Conner
> Supreme Court Justice

had a hot date and was hoping to get lucky. So, he counted up the register just a little early. Figuring that he would "ask" the last few customers in the store to pay with their ATM.

Once I figured out that he was lying to me, I gave myself permission to lie to him. I needed to give him a reason to reopen his register. I needed to give him a *want*. As you will learn later on with Law #2, people won't do shit unless they want to. So, I needed him to want to. I hadn't been on aisle 5, but I figured if I had broken a jar of mayo there he would want me to pay for it. And, if I only had cash he would figure out how to accept my money. I learned from his behavior what I needed to get my needs met (as well as Jazz's needs).

I'm pretty sure that if I had allowed myself to get all upset and throw a tantrum, I would have been acting like a jerk and he would have stuck to his lying words. If I had gotten pissed and stormed out of the store, he wouldn't have cared. He probably would have turned to the next person in line, and acting all hurt said, "Some people are so rude ... Ya have ta use your ATM card."

If you don't analyze every situation to learn the "known" rules and the "secret" rules you will bash your head up against the game of life.

[Just because it will "kill" my friends if you knew, the poker game that night was amazing. I kicked some righteous bootie.]

YOU CAN'T MAKE ME

I've never done the survey, but I think that one out of every hundred teens that reads the above, says, "Screw you, you can't make me. It's stupid. Life sucks. You suck!" If you're in the 99% group feel free to skip this section and move onto Law #2.

So, you're the one. You're that individual who believes that just because you're you, you don't have to deal with laws. However, you didn't donate this book to the library as I suggested earlier. So, there is still hope for you. I hope you're not reading this because you're locked up and it's better than staring at your cell mate as he passes gas. But, even if you are in jail, read on...

So, I ask myself, why are you continuing to read this *stupid* book. The answer is because you want better for yourself. Nothing fancy, you *want*. How human of you. Even if you don't like it, you are stuck with the fact that there are things more powerful than yourself.

I'm sure you "believe" in gravity. It's a physical law that no one has any say about. It *is* and we all have to deal with it. There are things that are outside of your control. There are rules in life that cannot be repealed; like the Law of Gravity. If Congress decided to repeal the Law of Gravity, put it to a vote and announced that the Law of Gravity was no more, what would happen? Any moron who believed that it was repealed would walk off a tall building and splat—one less moron. According to the strange folks at Darwin.com that kind of stuff occurs all the time. Morons bumping themselves off and cleaning up the human gene pool. (See Darwin.com for more information on how some fellow humans clean up the human gene pool.)

Responses may be altered by their effects on the environment
E.L. Thorndike

PEOPLE ARE CREATURES OF HABIT

I once watched a relatively intelligent person look for a stapler. She wanted to staple a few pages together for me. She opened and closed her desk drawer five times looking for the stapler.

"It's supposed to be right here," she muttered; each time getting a little more frustrated.

Now, think about this for a second. If you checked the drawer once or twice and the stapler wasn't there, why check it again? She checked because it was "supposed to be there." It wasn't, but she didn't let new facts get in the way of her beliefs. This seems crazy to me. If you keep doing the same thing over and over and keep getting the results you don't want, over and over again, that's crazy behavior. Why do it? It seems that anything you do that is not the same old behavior (the one you had proof didn't work) gives you a better chance of finding out what does work. If checking in the drawer has proven to be useless, then even standing on your head and reciting a poem would make more sense. Maybe you would notice the stapler under the couch. Since your way wasn't working, anything else has a minute chance of working.

The world is but a school of inquiry.

Michael de Montaigne

You have read all this crap for a reason. Maybe the reason is that you're tired of the way you are running your life. Maybe you are tired of how you are allowing others to run your life. Maybe you are so fearful of running your life that you can't even get started taking self control.

You're not alone. Even if you're one in a hundred, there are a lot of you. We have close to three hundred million people in this county. That's three million people that feel similar to the way you feel. Don't give up on yourself. Help is only pages away.

Family's always embarrassing isn't it?

Douglas Adams
The Restaurant at the End of The Universe

SUPERFLUITY

REID:

Through most of elementary and high school, I was a very poor student. Although I am perfectly capable of doing well in school, I saw the public education system as so incredibly flawed that it wasn't worth my effort. "This is crap," I told myself. I chose not to participate. Thinking somehow that the rules didn't apply to me, I thought of myself as something equivalent to a conscientious objector. I rejected school on principle, and I quietly snickered at my peers who tried and succeeded.

I have always been adept at absorbing knowledge; in fact, I love to learn. Some of my teachers related to me the strange phenomena of this quiet, unassuming kid who rarely turned in a piece of homework, yet who aced nearly every test thrown his way. In fact, I was proud of this. My reasoning at the time was that I could prove the system wrong by learning all there was to learn and at the same flunking spectacularly. If this could be done, I thought, it would prove that the point of it all was not to learn, but to satisfy some half-wit, far-removed, state official's idea of what an education should be. Perhaps I was right, but whom did I help? What did I change?

I realize now that however pointless the courses were, getting "A's" in them would have helped me toward my goal of getting into a university. I was stuck in high school whether I liked it or not, (I didn't) but it was my choice whether I wanted to use my time there as a stepping-stone for what I wanted. Junior college has been a wonderful second chance for me and I am finally enjoying school, (for the most part) but I wonder how much easier it would be for me right now if I hadn't slept through the last 12 years.

HOLLY:

What a way to learn a lesson. I ended up with a whole month of being grounded, and one week of suspension from school before I caught a glimpse of what this Life Law was all about.

I was a sophomore in high school and I decided to celebrate my Friday early by getting plastered in first period. Imagine this, a girl about 110 pounds; puking 100 proof Hot Damn all over a high school campus, totally shit-faced, people laughing at her, trying to get her to the toilet, the whole shebang. This was me at sixteen years old. My mom picked me up from the school, realized that I was drunk off my ass, and called the school to tell the "authorities" about my day of drunkenness. I, along with my friend, was totally busted. This is where this Life Law came into play.

I realized that it was not my place to go off and do whatever the hell I wanted to do. I figured out that there were rules only after I got pissed off, and threw my fit about being grounded and suspended. I knew that these were the rules; being under the influence, drinking or drugs would result in suspension. Drinking or drugs under the age of eighteen would result in being grounded for a month from everything but the bedroom. So, I dealt with it and learned from it.

This theory plays into a lot of different situations, work, school, home, family, driving, money, etc. In life there are rules, just as Dr. Phil says, and it is important to know those rules to get what you want out of life. Drinking at school got me nothing; no actually it got me negative nothing. So, I had to learn from this, and I did, though just like all teenagers it took me a couple of tries to figure out this Life Law, but I never did drink at school again.

Life's Law #2

People do what they are going to do

I feel so bad. I told our son that I would kill him if he used drugs!

It's OK honey, it wasn't you... It was the alcohol speaking.

© 1998 CopitchInc.com

2. LIFE'S LAW #2

People do what they are going to do

I would hate to be "normal." In fact, I take great offense at the fact that in so many ways I am normal. Don't get me wrong. I'm perfectly okay with my skin producing normal cells. I definitely don't want skin cancer. But when it comes to who I am, at my core, I think normal is boring.

Life Rule #2 is about normal; how people tend to act; how people usually behave. Normal behavior.

I have often said that I am very impressed with mankind, but that individual humans tend to be embarrassing. If advanced aliens show up one day to conquer earth, to enslave us like, say a cow, and incorporate us into their alien economy, that would really piss me off. Mankind is spectacular. We are creative beings at our infancy. I have great hope for us.

But, as individuals, even the brightest of us is petty. We tend to be selfish, narrow minded, and basically fearful beings. Even large groups can be selfish, narrow-minded, and basically fearful.

At the present time there are approximately 65 wars that are being waged on planet earth. Each of these wars is over something petty. "My god is better than your god." "Three hundred years ago your ancestors stole that piece of land from my ancestors." Or some such thing. I wonder what we would do if a giant interplanetary invasion force presented itself just off the moon, would we be warring amongst ourselves, or scared shitless? I think initially we would be overwhelmed, then we would organize and work together to protect ourselves.

This past week in my area of northern California there was a large forest fire that forced the evacuation of a mountain town some forty miles away. Homes were lost and lives were sent into upheaval. The local radio station announced that the local Red Cross needed money to help the fire victims. The next morning countless people drove by the Civic Center dropping off cash and canned food. In a few hours $25,000 and two and a half truck loads of food were donated. This happened the same week that the mill, ten miles south of here, announced that it was closing for good.

One of the families I worked with the day of the donation drive came into my office in great spirits. I was somewhat surprised because just the week before that same family was talking about how they had been fighting a lot at home ever since they found out that Dad was to be unemployed. Last week the stress in the family was eating them up from inside. This week the family was rejuvenated.

The oldest child, Adam, plopped on the couch and said, "We just dropped off $25 and a bag of groceries for the fire victims."

We human beings sure can be wonderful.

Didn't I just contradict myself? Are people petty or are people wondrous? Which one? Well, both. The same person can be wondrous in one situation and petty in another. Fair and even handed one moment and an irrational prick the next. This brings us to Rule #2, People do what they are going to do.

I don't care who we are talking about, your mom, the Pope, or the wino on Fifth and Plastered—they do what they are going to do. They react, feel, and do what they tend to have done in similar situations in the past. Humans are creatures of habit. To that extent we are individually predictable.

Understanding this predictability is how we start to uncover the secret rules of our friends, parents and teachers. It is our window into their real thoughts.

If your friend is always standing you up, or seems comfortable about being late, his behavior tells you something. His words may say, "That sounds great, I'll meet you at eight." But his behavior says. "I'll show up at eight, if nothing better shows up."

If your stud muffin says, "I think that women should get equal pay for equal work," he seems respectful of women. But if his hands say, "You're a piece of my property and I like what I own." You really know what he thinks of women.

All things being equal, believe the behavior.

TERRORISM

This book was outlined months before I actually sat down to write it. The section above was written one week before the terrorist attacks on the World Trade Center in New York City and the Pentagon in Virginia. These horrific terrorist acts have changed our basic understanding of our world. The terrorists destroyed an icon in New York and damaged another in Virginia while murdering close to three thousand people. They gave themselves permission to murder. But this was only the ugly part of the story. Through all the initial shock, I noticed an amazing part of this unbelievable tragedy.

I watched CNN as the first building burned. The commentators explained that there was no information about what caused this accident. Then came the overwhelming sight of the second commercial airliner slamming into the second tower. At that moment the world knew the first building was not an accident. A short time later came the report of the Pentagon being hit. Next a plane crashed in Pennsylvania. The world was going crazy. It was unraveling in front of our collective eyes.

Then it happened. CNN showed people below the first building in New York. The video documented one man helping another man in an ash filled street. The video was shot from the relative safety of a mini-mart store front. It showed a third man at a glass door watching the two men out in the debris ridden street. The man at the door of the store was holding the door closed as the devastation outside stormed by. The man at the door was horrified. He was rigid with panic. Then he ran out into the horror and helped. Within moments, three men came out of the gray cloud of death. All three helping each other. All covered with ash.

This scene was very meaningful for me to witness. At the beginning of this video clip there were three ethnically different types of people. At the end, there was one skin color—ash. In a way, I saw the aliens attack and we became one. One person helping another for one good reason, *it seemed like the right thing to do*. People are amazing creatures.

YOU ARE A PEOPLE TOO

Up to now I have been talking about others. How they act. But the same is true for you. You are also a creature of habit. You also have set reactions to particular situations. You too are predictable. You do what you are going to do.

If you say, "I want to go to college." But your behavior says, "TV first, homework never!" Believe the behavior.

If your words say, "I'll be back at nine, Mom." When you know your ride clearly told you he wasn't leaving this party until midnight or one. And then you show up at one thirty with that same old sorry ass story, "Joel refused to leave, what could I do, he was my ride!" Believe your behavior. You are comfortable lying to your mother.

All things being equal, you are going to do what you are going to do.

PEOPLE DO WHAT WORKS

In 1911, E.L. Thorndike first explained the **Law of Effect**. Thorndike showed that when learning, *responses may be altered by their effects on the environment*. What this means in plain speak is that behaviors (responses) that lead to positive outcomes (as defined by you) are increased, and behaviors that lead to negative outcomes (as defined by you) are decreased. Simply, Thorndike noted what we all know. If something works for us, we do it again. If it doesn't work for us, we stop doing it.

"People do what works," is a little statement with a shit load of power for you to grab and use. What I am talking about is that everyone does what works for them. Not sometimes—every time.

At first many people throw this truth back at me and say things like:

"That seems a little harsh. You're telling me that I'm fat because I want to be fat?

"You're saying I'm flunking Algebra because I want to flunk Algebra?"

"You're saying I want to be shy?"

"That sounds stupid. You mean I'm choosing to have my parents treat me like I'm a little kid?"

Yep! That's what I'm saying. On purpose or by accident, you influence how others treat you and how you treat yourself. I know it is common nowadays to blame something or someone other than yourself. But that sounds like denial to me. I watched a doctor on TV explain that due to the pain in our inner child Americans are overweight. We are trying to nurture ourselves by being our own mothers breast. What psycho-babble. I heard a psychologist on the radio explain that because birthing is so hard on the newborn's psyche we all need to be channeled and re-birthed. A lady on an infomercial told me that our wrinkled skin was not age related, it was due to toxins from poor nutrition and poor emotional energy. For only hundreds of dollars she would sell me a meditation tape and food supplements to fix me right up. To this I say: "bullshit!"

There is a billion dollar industry teaching Americans that it is not their fault that something bad happened to them. It is usually called the Self Empowerment Industry or the Supplement Industry. I call it: Lie To Them And Take Their Money Industry.

I understand why people are paying to be told that they are victims. It's easier than taking self responsibility. But, I believe that we are really harming ourselves and our society. The truth is simple and boringly factual. People do what works. Period.

Would you do anything that didn't work for you? We are creatures of reward and punishment. Reward increases behavior, punishment decreases behavior. It's that simple. People work to reward themselves and work hard to avoid punishment. But, there are many levels of personal reward and punishment, read on.

Sally was a binge drinker. For the last four months she had been getting plastered almost every Friday and Saturday night. She told her group home house mother that she wanted to see me because her friend said, "He's pretty funny!" When the house mother set up the appointment with me she told me that Sally was a little depressed but a nice kid. She also told me that Sally was removed from her single mothers home when her mom was jailed for methamphetamine sales.

When Sally came into my office she seemed like a great kid with a lot of social skills. She had friends, got good grades, and had future goals. She seemed like she was doing well considering her situation. About halfway through our first session I asked her, "Why are you *really* here."

If you can't see the reward, you're not looking hard enough!

"I'm pregnant," she snapped coldly.

Over the next fifteen minutes she told me about how she was spending Friday and Saturday nights drunk. Her mom had been out of jail for the last six months. And, for the last four months, she had been allowed by the county social worker to have home visits Friday after school to Sunday early evening. The social worker's goal was for her to live with her mom by the end of the summer. Sally explained that during the first weekend of home visits her mom told her that she didn't think it was fair. Mom was upset with Sally for interfering with her weekend fun. So, mom told Sally that as long as she didn't tell anyone or get into trouble she could do what she wanted all weekend. "She told me," Sally said, "As long as you're doing good in school, your weekends are yours."

Sally was spending the weekends drinking with the younger men in her mom's apartment complex.

She said in a whisper, "I must have had sex when I was passed out."

She wasn't sure exactly when. She reported passing out at least one night most weekends. Sally was fifteen.

Over the next few weeks Sally kept blaming everyone for her problems. She was furious with the county social worker. She was upset with her group home. She hated men for using her. She was pissed with her mom's boyfriend for letting her mom drink. When I explained that I thought that people do what works, I was elevated to the top of the list of people she hated because I kept suggesting that she was involved in her own life.

She initially refused to look at her involvement in her problems. Over time she taught me (and herself) that at first she was happy that her mother thought she was mature enough to take care of herself on weekends. Initially she really liked the freedom and the attention from the men in the apartment building. She truly liked getting over on the controlling county social worker and the nosey house mother. She loved the feeling of the alcohol

Be a good animal, true to your instincts.

D.H. Lawrence

and freedom from her thoughts that the alcohol gave her.

As time went on she worried that her mom didn't really care about her and that mom only wanted to enjoy her weekends. Sally worried that if the county social worker found out what she was doing she would put her mother back in jail. She figured that booze was much better for her mom than meth.

Two sessions later she summed it all up:

"I knew I was being passed around and screwed by lots of men. But I kept telling myself that it was only fair. It made me feel nothing. It was my way of saying that my mom didn't deserve me, and when I was dead she would know how terrible a mom she was. I hate her so much I hate me. I just didn't have the guts to kill myself."

Rewards are not always understood or a positive. Often when people do something that they really don't want to do, the reward is hidden and painful. We have to reward undesirable behaviors or we wouldn't do that to ourselves. We have to understand what works for us, and why it works for us, to get control over ourselves.

Sally's reward system was so complicated that she needed therapy to sort out what she was doing to herself. I use her case as an example of how hard you might have to work to understand your personal system of rewards.

Let's look at a few common "hidden" reward situations:

"That seems a little harsh. You're telling me that I'm fat because I want to be fat?

It is very common for food to be used as an instant reward system in our society. Many people reward themselves with food whenever a sad thought crosses their mind.

"You're saying I'm flunking Algebra because I want to flunk Algebra?"

Often girls earn bad grades in junior and senior high school because boys don't like smart girls. People do a lot to be popular.

Regularly people earn poor grades in school because they do not have the self confidence to tell a teacher "I don't get it."

Recently a lineman for a high school football team told me that he didn't get sixth grade math, so why bother with ninth grade math. He was planning to have a team of accountants that watched over his money when he turned pro. His future hope gave him permission not to look at his present reality—he needed help in math.

"Your saying I want to be shy?"

Shy must be working for you or you would be building your outgoing skills.

"That sounds stupid. You mean I'm choosing to have my parents treat me like I'm a little kid?"

Sure, you have a lot of influence on others, especially your parents. Read on!

YOU INFLUENCE HOW OTHERS TREAT YOU

I once did a weekend seminar for one of those big companies that can afford to advertise during the Olympics or the Super Bowl. The seminar was devoted to helping middle managers learn how to motivate their sales force. One Saturday morning I was surprised to find a room full of bright eyed, white-starched-shirt-wearing, power-tie-toting, middle aged men. I had just crawled out of bed, showered under a tiny water saver shower-head, and had not yet had any coffee. It was 8:30 AM and my day was only thirty minutes old. The men in the audience were awake. Happily awake. I was disgusted. To me, the only way I could be happy at 8 AM was if I was up to deliver my wife's baby. Saturday mornings are for sleeping, everyone knows that (except during youth soccer season).

I talked to the group about my plan for the day and pointed out a few goals and objectives. I asked if there were any questions and waited for some. I have talked to hundreds of parent groups, teacher groups and therapist groups. Someone always has a question. This group looked fearful. It dawned on me that this group wasn't expecting to participate. They thought they were there to listen and absorb information. Boy, were they in for a big surprise!

I called on people. "What is your biggest problem with your work force?" "How do you motivate people to work?" "Tell me your biggest thorns-in-your-side and who put them there?" Finally, after some fifteen minutes, one older gentleman stood up and growled, "Well DOCTOR, I have to spend my weekend here, are you going to tell me how to find employees who will follow directions... I need winners! Where do I find them!?" Then he crossed his arms

The need to be right—the sign of a vulgar mind.
                                        Albert Camus

and plopped himself into his chair. The room became alive with murmuring. It seemed that this man had shared a common problem for the attendees. I was so excited. Anger. Pure and simple anger. An emotion I could work with. What a wonderful opportunity. So, I told a story (I'm a cognitive behavioral therapist—I always tell stories).

> A couple of months ago I was at Sea World. I saw the dolphin show. This gray sleek mammal leaped out of the pool, did a forward flip over a bright red nylon rope, and dove back into the water. What a sight!
> A small boy in front of me asked his grandfather, "How did they teach the dolphin to do that?" The grandfather said, "They go out into the ocean and scare the dolphins out of the water with their big boat engines. The ones that jump the highest they capture and bring here for the show."

This was an intriguing theory, but not an accurate one. I postulated the boy's question to my hostile audience: "How do you teach a dolphin to jump over a rope?" I ask you the same question, "How would you teach a dolphin to jump over a rope?"

The most common answer to the question was, "I'd hang a fish from a rope above the water." The problem with this is how do you get the dolphin to look up at the fish? Dolphins don't go around in their natural environment, looking up out of the water, expecting mackerel. Most fish don't jump out of the ocean. And, even the motivated ones that do, would not be enough to fill the bellies of many a dolphin.

The way you teach a dolphin to jump is by using a process called **shaping**. Shaping is the process of rewarding a behavior each time it gets closer and closer to the desired behavior. You can't go out into the ocean with a loud speaker attached to your boat yelling, "Jump! Jump! Come on Flipper, JUMP!" You won't get a dolphin to jump out of the water, do a back flip, smile at the camera and come to the boat to be captured. If you did, you would have what corporate middle managers call a "WINNER!" It just doesn't happen. At first, dolphins don't know anything about show biz.

Dolphins are not fools. They are readily willing to investigate their world and find food. That is their job. At first you have to get the dolphin to recognize the importance of the rope. If you place the rope in the pool so the dolphin can swim above it and below it they will do just that. When the dolphin "accidently" swims above the rope you drop a fish in the pool. After a few chance encounters

For those of you taking
psychology classes.

Operant Conditioning:

*Negative Reinforcer:
The removal of an ad-
verse stimulus that in-
creases the likelihood of
a response. A reward.*

*Positive Reinforcer: A
stimulus that increases
the likelihood of a re-
sponse. A reward.*

*Punishment: The pre-
sentation of an adverse
stimulus following an un-
desired response that de-
creases the likelihood of
the undesired response.*

*Extinction: The process
in which a learned re-
sponse is no longer re-
inforced, reverting to its
preconditioned level.*

*Successive Approxi-
mation (Shaping): The
process of rewarding for
a behavior each time it
gets closer and closer to
the desired behavior.*

*Modeling: A hands on
form of shaping behavior.
It is learning by imita-
tion.*

the dolphin says to itself, "Hmm...
I think there is an interesting relationship here. Something is going
on between that lifeless piece of
seaweed and a fish falling from the
heavens. I'll call that new kind of
plant, hmm... rope. Now let's see, if
I swim under the rope nothing happens. But, if I swim over the rope,
lunch. This I can live with. In fact, I
feel encouraged to keep swimming
above the rope."

Then the trainer raises the
rope. Just a little each time. Not
to be mean, but making it harder
for our friend Flipper. It's just not
much of a show if the rope is in the
water. Spectators would say, "Big
deal, the dolphin can swim at the
top of the pool." You're not going
to get $14.50 a head for a dolphin
fin poking out of the water playing
shark! The trainer keeps raising
the rope slowly, over time, until it
is well above the water.

Your parents did the same
thing to you. If your mom wanted to
teach 18 month old you to politely
say, "Excuse me mother, could I
please have a piece of toast?" She
couldn't wait until you were completely verbalizing your needs. If
mom waited that long, you would
have ended up one skinny ass dead
kid. That's not good!

What Mom wanted to do was
to shape your behavior. Mom said,
"Do you want toast? Toast, toast,
toast?" Then one day you said, "Ta
Ta Ta" for toast and Mom got all
excited. She may have called Dad.
She may have even had him get off
the couch. She probably made you
say "Ta ta ta" all over again. Kind of
like a really cheap home version of

dolphins jumping out of the water. Mom got out the video camera. She called the grandparents. Your mom declared you to be a genius. But, if at age 16, you started saying, "Ta Ta Ta" for toast, she'd have your urine checked for street drugs.

Your mom rewarded as she caught you making progress. "Ta Ta Ta," worked for a while. But, in no time, "Ta Ta peas" was needed. Then "toes peas" was changed to "toast please."

This is shaping. Some psychologists call it *successive approximation*. Shaping behavior accounts for the vast majority of complex learned behaviors such as how people treat you and how you treat others.

Through shaping, you influence the world and the world influences you.

LAW #1 AND LAW #2 IN THE REAL WORLD

Conner had just turned sixteen. He knew about the birthday party that his mother and three sisters were planning for him. He didn't want to participate. Three months prior, his parents had a huge argument in the living room. It went on for forty-five minutes. It was about money. It always was about money.

Conner had lain in bed with his pillow over his head trying to drown out the hate. The house got quiet. His bedroom door flung open knocking things off the dresser. His father looked crazed. He was red faced and breathing through enlarged nostrils. His father bellowed, "You're the man of the family now! I can't live with your devil possessed mother! We're getting a divorce." He slammed the door with so much force that the door frame splintered. As his father drove away with a screech, Conner went to console his weeping mother. He told her, "It'll be okay in a day or two. Dad will calm down."

Conner's mother turned on him with all her rage. "Your father's a bastard. Let him go live with that whore of a secretary."

Weeks after this major blow up, Conner said to me, "They were arguing about money. They always argue about money. He's an elder in our church. Everyone knows about my dad ... I've lost everything. I have nowhere to show my face." Conner didn't know about the affair. His world was shattered.

Conner used Law #1 and Law #2 to help deal with his family's ongoing crisis. He knew that he had to get his mind around the fact that his parents were getting a divorce. He had no choice but to deal with the fact that his parents were out of control and he couldn't hope this problem away. He had to deal with the changes around the house. His father was living in a hotel, refusing to talk with anyone. His mother was sitting on the couch, crying twenty-four hours a day. His sisters were constantly bickering with each other. He wanted it all to stop.

He also knew that he had no control about how others were going to deal with this crisis. But, he wanted to help, to do something. He decided to ask advice from his mothers best friend. She seemed to be an understanding woman. Conner and Mrs. Powell worked it out that the girls all got invited to friends' houses for a few days. This way they could each get emotional support from their friends' families.

He would stay home and watch over his mother. His aunt would stay with her when he was at school. He knew that he needed to get out of the house and at school he would be able to stop thinking about his problems for at least a few minutes every period.

Conner proved to be an amazing support system for his family. He also took care of himself, by taking care of his family.

Nicky, newly fifteen, had no friends at her very stuck up private school. She knew people, but she had no real friends, only acquaintances. When I asked her why she thought she had no friends she hemmed and hawed about the rest of the student body being stuck up or dumb, but in no time she got to the fact that, "I have a very morbid sense of humor. Others just don't like my jokes." As it turned out, Nicky pushed people away with her mouth. Her specific skill was associating others stories with her "gross" stories. Her family was all "fire people." Six of the nine family members that she spent most of her time with were emergency personnel with the fire department. The rest were "married to the department." She had spent her entire life hearing stories about death, destruction, and auto accidents. She was so used to it, she was never shocked at the family dinner table when someone talked about the latest victim he had scraped off the highway.

After a brief overview of Life's Law #1 and #2 she suggested that she should only talk about what the kids at school talked about. I assured her that her fellow students had a short memory and she could probably find things to talk about that never made the front page of the paper. Three days later she met Sondra, a popular girl in second period English. They had a lot in common. They both liked school. They both liked their families. And they were both sure that boys were immature slugs with bad breath and active hands.

Two weeks later:

Nicky: I got invited to a party on a huge houseboat. It was great, Sondra's family was so nice. It was almost heaven.

Dr. Phil: Almost heaven?

Nicky:	Almost, her family talks a lot about money. Her dad is a stockbroker. Her mom sells real estate. They talk money non stop. Sondra's so funny, she said, "Christmas is the worst. The uncles come over and fight about the new changes in the tax law."
Dr. Phil:	Have you talked to Sondra about the fire department stuff?
Nicky:	Sure. After a couple of days. She loves the stories. She said I should write a book ... maybe write a movie. Her dad said I could be a millionaire. Her mom offered to find me a mansion to buy. See what I mean, her family likes me!
Dr. Phil:	How about the other kids at school?
Nicky:	Most are boring. Lots of makeup and clothes gab. The same stuff everyday. But I'm not talking about the dead stuff and people are treating me like I'm in the room.
Dr. Phil:	You planning to run for class president?
Nicky:	That's not funny Dr. Phil. I want to *survive* at the zoo, I'm definitely not getting too close to the animals.

Nicky's problem was painful for her, but it took less than a week to get it under her control. Once she used Life's Law #1 and #2, she empowered herself to get her needs met.

SUPERFLUITY

HOLLY:

This was a tough law for me to learn. I am one to give my advice on a dime, even if people don't really want to hear it. I have learned so much throughout my life that I feel that what I have to say means something and should be heard.

My biological father moved to Alaska when I was 14 years old. We never really had a great relationship, though through the years he called me when things were good in his life, to tell me and make me think that he was finally on the right track. I always fell for his stories and thought that he had changed from when I had seen him last. We talked about every three months, and he would never call if there was a failing in his life. He would always have a new job, and was still trying to stop drinking. Things were always the same. I had hopes though because of the sound of his voice or the words he would say, the lies that he would tell me to make me think that he was an okay person, though he was still the same old man, drowning himself in his beer because life had wronged him in so many ways.

One night he called me, I could tell that he had been drinking because of the volume of his voice and the belligerent sentences that slurred out of his mouth. He was calling to tell me that he was thinking about committing suicide. He went on and on about how he had screwed up being a dad and was a lousy person just by sight. For about an hour he spilled his soul into my ear and I was astonished. I couldn't believe that a father would call his 18-year-old daughter and tell her this. So, I tried to talk the old man through this, telling him that if he had really wanted to do it so badly he would have just done it and only left his body behind to be found, he would not have called me. I was being the devil's advocate in a way and jabbing him with the words that he didn't want to hear. I was not going to fall for this game. He wanted pity and that was all. He wanted to hear that I would be losing something if he did this, though in reality I wasn't going to miss a thing. Like I said earlier, we never had a great relationship. We never had another conversation after this.

He didn't take his own life, but about a year later I found out that he had taken the life of another. This was a selfish act, just as the last phone conversation was between us, and now he is where he deserves to be.

Dr. Phil states in this chapter, "Humans are creatures of habit. To that extent we are individually predictable." Here I learned full force that people will do what they are going to do, no matter what kind of advice or time you give them. I waited 18 years for my father to change, and I now see that it was a waste of time because people will do what they are going to do. It was only a matter of time before he completely brought himself down, along with anyone else he could. He was trying to bring me down with him, but I knew better than to fall for his games.

REID:

The phrase "People are going to do what they're going to do" rings especially true for me. I tend to be a particularly self-critical person and I have a number of personality traits and behaviors that I look upon as "bad." After reading this chapter, I realized that if I've been lazy, it's because lazy has usually worked for me. If my people skills are lacking, it's because I haven't really felt the need to be social. Up until now I've been able to get my needs met, to get my wants satisfied without ever needing to confront these deficits. I am at an age where I'm about to be thrust into the "real world," whatever that means, properly equipped or not. It is only now that I realize how much I need to change in order to get what I want.

Life's Law #3

You are 100% responsible
for dealing with your life

"According to my survey, not one single inmate in
your prison is guilty of a damn thing!"

3. LIFE'S LAW #3

You are 100% responsible
for dealing with your life

Over the years Life's Law #3 has produced the most arguments with the new adults I work with. On the surface people are comfortable with this law, as long as they read 100% as 93% or 97%. So let me make this clear, you are **100%** responsible for how you deal with your life.

Carlos was in big trouble with the law. He was seventeen and arrested for shooting a fourteen year old boy. If that wasn't bad enough, when the cops searched him he had a pocketful of rock cocaine. Carlos' attorney asked me to look in on him to see if I could come up with anything helpful for his legal defense.

Carlos had been in jail four months when I first met him. He was handcuffed and dressed in an orange jump suit. You didn't need to be a shrink to understand his mannerisms. He was pissed.

As it turned out, Carlos was being unjustly accused. He explained that the cops were out to get him and the kid he shot deserved it. Carlos was positive he was the victim. What was most confusing to Carlos' attorney was that he couldn't get Carlos to stop confessing to the crimes. He told everybody. Even people who didn't ask.

> Man it's like this. This *punta* came into the hood and he should know better than scope my house for his joy. He just tipped on down the street and flashed me as a nobody. So I had no choice. I didn't want to, ya know ... so I capped him. I even did him a favor. I only put one hole in his lost ass. He made me, ya know ... I ain't got nothin' against him or nothin'. I even pray for him to get better and to get some sense. If he don't learn, next time he going to get himself killed.

On the subject of the rock cocaine in his pocket:

> It ain't like I use the stuff. My body is a temple ya know. A little beer with the boys, I ain't saying I'm a saint or nothin'. The Man don't believe me. Sticking me with Possession with Intent, that's bullshit and he knows it. I was just holding it for a

friend. You can ask anyone, I stopped using that shit long ago...

I wasn't much help to Carlos' attorney, but this situation does point out an interesting fact; people lie to themselves about their responsibility to their life.

I assume most of us see that Carlos was responsible for what got him into jail. How about Lisa's story?

Lisa had been sent home from school three times in two weeks for *showing her midriff.* I was seeing her family due to the divorce of her parents. Lisa was very upset with the school for not letting her dress with style.

Lisa: It's not fair. Even my mother thinks it's fashionable. It's not like I'm dressing like a slut.

Dr. Phil: Did the principal call you a slut?

Lisa: No. He just gives you a copy of the rules and says that all students must follow them. But, I'm dressed tastefully, I'm not revealing too much.

Lisa's mother was trying to be supportive of Lisa and she agreed that Lisa wasn't inappropriately dressed. In fact, she was thinking about suing the school for embarrassing her daughter by implying that she was a slut.

What do you think? Was Lisa taking 100% responsibility for how she dealt with her life?

Nope, not 100% in my opinion.

Dr. Phil: Why do you go to high school?

Lisa: I want to be a nurse and help people.

Dr. Phil: The days that you were sent home, did you work towards your goal of being a nurse so you could help people?

Lisa: No, but I'm going to do the work that I missed during Saturday School.

Dr. Phil: Does the shirt the school required you to wear get in the way of your learning?

Lisa: No.

Dr. Phil: So how come you are making such a big deal about your clothes all of a sudden?

Pick your battles

A long quiet minute later. In a low voice:

Lisa: I like the attention of the stupid boys.

At that moment, Lisa took 100% responsibility for her high school world. If getting the attention of the stupid boys was more important than getting her education, I guess she should have gone to school butt naked. Until she was arrested she would have definitely gotten the attention of most of the school (Maybe even some of the smart boys). If the reason Lisa was going to school was to become a nurse and help people, then her goal forces her to take a particular life path. Our goals force paths upon us. You can't get into a nursing program if you can't get a good high school education.

Taking 100% responsibility for dealing with your life is hard. It is multifaceted. It is often a pain in the ass. It would be much easier if you just got to blame others.

The American Heritage Dictionary defines responsibility as:

Involving personal accountability or ability to act without guidance or superior authority. Able to make moral or rational decisions on one's own and therefore answerable for one's behavior.

So, if you don't get the grade you want on the exam, you are 100% responsible for how you deal with it. If a girl stands you up, you are 100% responsible for how you deal with it. If your parents are hard to live with, you are 100% responsible for how you deal with it. If your car gets stolen, you are 100% responsible for how you deal with it.

At this point some smart individual likes to throw me a zinger. "You mean if a girl gets raped or my mother gets shot by a gang banger, they're responsible?"

I say yes! You are always 100% responsible for how you deal with it. Read on...

RESPONSIBILITY DOES NOT MEAN BLAME

Responsibility is a person's accountability. When I was fourteen, my friend Bigbird (a name not given by his parents) threw an ice ball at my head. It missed me by half an inch, luckily for my noggin. It hit the window of our school with laser accuracy. I laughed as the ice ball flew by. Tenths of a second later, I worried if Bigbird was going to be roasted alive by our humorless principal.

Bigbird was responsible for breaking the window and the principal made that very clear as he growled at us in his office. But, to my surprise, the principal didn't <u>blame</u> Bigbird for the accident. Everyone knew that Bigbird was clumsy. Everyone knew that Bigbird was a follower. So, can you guess what happened? The damn principal blamed me!

"Mr. Copitch, you need to take greater responsibility for your horseplay. Mr. Cleveland (Bigbird) looks up to you. I expect more out of you. It is inconceivable how someone with your potential can end up in my office so often." (It went on from there for another twenty minutes!)

I was dead meat. You know you're dead meat when you get called Mister by an authority figure. The principal was correct however. Bigbird did look up to me, even if he was twelve inches taller than I was (he was also as skinny as a post, but what a great guy). The fact was that I had set Bigbird up. I *was* to blame. I plastered Bigbird in the thigh with a slush ball. He ran after me to get even. I ran in front of the school office's picture window because I knew no one was dumb enough to throw a snowball at the front of the school. I was wrong.

In this use of the word, blame is the state of being culpable. I deserved the blame because I caused a wrong. Bigbird caused an accident. He was responsible for an accident. I was to blame because my behavior was an intentional act.

Let's look at this in a more serious situation. Stephanie was molested when she was six years old. She didn't tell anyone because her uncle was the molester. She was very confused and deeply blamed herself for many years. She came to my office when she was twenty-four years of age. She had recently told the man she loved that she could not marry him. But, she could not tell him the reason why—Stephanie was afraid to have sex. This was not a huge problem while she was dating. Both of them were saving themselves for marriage. But she knew that she could not go on a honeymoon. You can't save yourself for marriage <u>after</u> you say "I do." At that point you have to "do." It took a lot of courage for Stephanie to reach out for help.

Over the course of a year, Stephanie worked very hard in therapy to combat her fears. During our last session, I asked her to sum up her therapy experience.

> I learned that my uncle was to blame for be-
> traying my trust in him and that I was not respon-

sible for being a victim at the age of six. But, I am responsible now if I feel like a six year old victim at the age of twenty-five.

After a long pause she continued.

I also know that if I let my life get ruined because of my past, that would be my fault. I am 100% responsible for how I deal with my life! I want a family. I deserve a family. And, I'm looking forward to getting pregnant.

We both cried with joy because we both knew that she was a powerful woman who understood Life's Law #3.

YOU ARE 100% RESPONSIBLE FOR DEALING WITH HOW OTHERS TREAT YOU

Most people assume that they have little, if any, control over how others treat them. I believe the opposite to be true. I believe that you are 100% responsible for dealing with how others treat you. That doesn't mean that you have 100% control of how others act. It simply means that you are responsible for how you deal with how they act towards you.

Recently a friend and I went out for our normal late Tuesday night dinner. Usually the restaurant is almost empty. This particular night the place was a mad house. It was packed with fire fighters just off the fire lines thirty miles away. The two waitresses were running all over, frantically trying to get the loud hungry mass fed.

The bus boy noticed us and said he would clean a table for us in a few minutes. My friend and I sat reading the menu. He said, "We're never getting served today!"

"It'll be OK," I said.

When the waitress made her way to our table she looked like she had been put through a blender. Her hair was a mess, her little purple decorative apron was stained and she seemed all jittery.

"Wow, you seem to be really overworked tonight. Are you OK.?" I inquired.

"Hungry ... rude ... fire fighters," She gasped. "They all want steak at the same time." She wiped her brow with her forearm.

She told us that since four o'clock the place had been packed

A liar that speaks the truth is not believed

Chinese Proverb

with hungry fire fighters. The kitchen was not set up for cooking this many steaks at one time and two wait-resses were not enough.

"It sounds unfair how you're being treated. When you have a min-ute for me let me know." I said.

"No, it's OK. What do you want? I'll get it for you. I don't care if they starve!" She said with a smile.

We were taken care of very well. The reason was because I treated the waitress with respect and empathy. I let her feel like a nice person and she subsequently acted towards me like a nice person. I'm sure that she was choosing to treat my table nicely, because she surely had no trouble growling at the loud table in the far corner.

As you go through your world you need to take responsibility for getting your needs met. If I was grumpy with the overworked waitress I would have been seen by her as one of the loud mass of humanity that filled her restaurant. But, recognizing that she was being put upon by her situation let her see me as a nice guy she wanted to feed. We both won. She felt appreciated, I got fed.

WHAT DO YOU PRESENT TO THE WORLD?

I told the above story to a sixteen year old boy who had been referred to my office because of his argumentative nature in school.

Benjamin: It's not fair. If I go into a restaurant and the waitress is having a bad day, she has no right to treat me like shit. She works for me, doesn't she?

Dr. Phil: I guess she works for you, but she is a person, isn't she?

Benjamin: So ... she's a person with a job. I shouldn't have to kiss her ass just for her to do her job.

Dr. Phil: Is that what I was doing, kissing ass?

Benjamin: Most definitely. 'You're working hard.' 'You're being mistreated!' He mimicked. She shouldn't take a job she didn't want. She is getting paid to get food for people and not to bitch.

Dr. Phil: I'll give you that what you are saying is true. But, none of that really matters to me. I wasn't nice to her because I had to be nice to her. I was nice to her because I wanted to be. In fact, I wanted to be served food in a timely manner. And, I didn't want her to growl at me. I was getting my needs met. It was also nice for the waitress, but that wasn't the reason I went to the restaurant, to be nice to a waitress. I went to the restaurant to get dinner. The way I interacted with the waitress got my needs met.

Benjamin: Oh, that's great for you with all your *psychology*. But I run into people that dump on me all the time.

Dr. Phil: Like at school?

Benjamin: Right. My first period teacher is a bitch to everyone. She doesn't care if I'm tired or if I have a headache. She just is on me, "Where's your homework," "Don't talk to me with that attitude!" I hate her and she knows it. So she takes any opportunity to jump on my back.

Dr. Phil: You mean if you turned in your homework, and were talking to her politely, she'd complain?

Benjamin: No. Of course not. She would probably find someone else to bitch at.

Dr. Phil: So, you're saying you're involved with her bitching at you?

Benjamin: I didn't say that, she just hates me.

Dr. Phil: It sounds to me that she will find someone else to hate if you don't fuel her fire by not turning in your homework.

Benjamin: Yeah, I guess. But, she works for me and she just bitches at me.

Dr. Phil: Let me understand this. Your teacher works for you? Her job is to get you to learn stuff? She thinks that *you* doing *your* homework will help you learn? It sounds like you have a pretty good employee for first period.

Benjamin: (with a smile) I hate when you make this all my stuff.

It was Benjamin's job to learn. Instead of taking that responsibility on his own shoulders, it was easier for him to blame his teacher. In fact, it was easier for him to blame his mother, his ex-girlfriend, and his grandparents for the problems in his life. He was the king of blaming others for his crappy relationships. It wasn't until he started to take personal responsibility for how he treated others and how others treated him, that his life became rewarding.

It is not until you accept 100% responsibility for dealing with your life that you will start to have a positive influence on how you treat others and others treat you.

SUPERFLUITY

REID:

I think we all struggle with this one. It is ridiculously easy to blame other people for our own actions and behaviors and just as hard to take responsibility for them. We've all seen those people go on Oprah, or Ricki, or any of those identical and equally awful daytime talk shows, and blame everything that's gone wrong in their life on their horrible parents. I often find myself scrambling to find someone else to put the blame on, rather than admitting I've made a mistake, only to realize that there's nobody but myself to be mad at and there's nothing to do but try and fix it.

HOLLY:

Put bluntly-I had a pretty shitty childhood. I had a father who was an alcoholic/crankster who beat the shit out of my mom in front of me for the first seven years of my life. He left. Then, I had a controlling step dad who molested me when I was twelve. He was found not guilty when put in front of a jury.

For so long I went back and forth first blaming them and then myself for all my insecurities and flaws and dwelt on the fact that I didn't have a "Leave It To Beaver" up bringing. I fell into drugs, hard-core, thinking that I would be able to forget the past, using the assholes that called themselves "Dad" as excuses to be doped up on anything I could get my hands on. Then I realized that I could take this one of two ways: 1) be a junkie the rest of my life running away from my problems with drugs, always blaming my faults and anything that went wrong in my life on those idiots. Or 2) go through the pain of never having a dad as opposed to the sperm donor father I had, and go on with my life knowing that at my age it wasn't my fault. I figure that I had no control over the situations I was put in. I could only become stronger from what I've seen and been through. That is a lot to swallow at 19, but I am glad with my decision and know strongly that I am better than both of them because they are still doing now what I chose not to do, blame others for their actions. They are simply lying to themselves.

Life's Law #4

Control
your own self-talk

"Even if I get Alzheimer's,
I'll remember what you just said!"

4. LIFE'S LAW #4

Control your own self-talk

Self-talk is shrink speak for the stuff that goes on in our heads that only we can hear. It is that internal dialogue that we keep with ourselves. Most of us do not really think about how we talk to ourselves—it just happens. But, self-talk is really important to understand if you wish to win in the game of life.

IT'S NOT BY CHANCE

There are hundreds or even thousands of ways to say almost anything. A simple statement like, "I'm going to the store," can be said:

> I'm history on the way to the store.
>
> Let me take leave of you. I am off to the store.
>
> I don't want to go ... but I have to go to the store.
>
> How come I have to go to the store?

It isn't by chance that you state things in a particular way. It is shaped by experience. Through interactions with others and education we learn to communicate. This probably is no secret to you. But, how about how you talk to yourself? This too is shaped by experience and education.

Aaron told me that he hated math. He was a "C" student in math because he hated it so much.

Dr. Phil: How do you know that you hate math?

Aaron: I don't know, I just do.

Dr. Phil: Do you hate money?

Aaron: No man, I work hard for my money.

Dr. Phil: If you got ripped on your paycheck, would you explain the mistake to your boss and get the right amount?

Aaron: Sure would. That happened to me once. Eighteen dollars. I got it the next pay period.

Dr. Phil:	Sounds to me that you like math when it has a dollar sign in front of it.
Aaron:	I guess I like that kind of math.
Dr. Phil:	But you just said you hated math.
Aaron:	Yeah, I guess I do ... but not money math.

Without realizing it, Aaron tells himself over and over that he doesn't like math. But really, he doesn't like some math. I bring this up because Aaron is constantly cutting himself down in his own mind. A little cut, over and over. I would think it is hard for Aaron to get motivated to go home and choose to do math homework when he *knows* that he hates math. But, it might be a little easier for Aaron if he hated some math, but not all math. Telling himself the truth, that math wasn't 100% negative, would help him to deal with math homework.

Self-talk is powerful. It comes from inside you. It comes from your past. It is a CD playing a familiar tune. If the tune is negative, it is hurtful in a negative way. If the tune is positive, it is helpful in a positive way.

Unfortunately, we are hard-wired to remember the negative better than the positive. Our brain lays down stronger negative memories than positive ones. Most people find that they can remember the negative events, the painful ones of their youth, more clearly than their positive memories.

It is common for people to recall in vivid detail the fall from a bike that sent them to the hospital. They can recall the street, the hospital, the words the doctor said. "You'll need a cast on that. That's one of the worst breaks I've ever seen." These same people probably can't tell you much about their fourth grade teacher or classmates.

This makes perfect sense from the evolutionary understanding of memory. It is more important for a person to learn from a life threatening injury so that type of situation can be avoided. If we don't learn from danger, we limit our chances to be around to carry on the species. We are hard wired to survive.

Our society tends to look at stuff from the negative. The sky is "partly cloudy" versus "partly sunny." We control our traffic intersec-

He who can not communicate his ideas, stands at the same level as he who has no ideas.

Pericles
Greek statesman

tions with "stop lights" versus "go lights." Negativity is powerful and easier to remember. We tend to talk to ourselves through negative thoughts. "I lost only one pound this week" versus, "I enjoyed a brisk walk four times this week. Next week I will walk five days out of seven. One pound a week is pretty good. In one hundred and twenty-seven weeks I'll be invisible!"

SELF-TALK CAN BE IMPLANTED

A lot of our self-talk is accidently implanted. It is given to us by others we feel are powerful in our lives. Moms, dads, teachers, friends, to name a few, give us information about ourselves that we lay down as powerful memories.

"My mother always said I was evil, that's why I dropped out of school." Judith told me.

Dr. Phil: Evil? That sounds mean.

Judith: I don't think she was mean, she just worried about me a lot.

Dr. Phil: What does evil mean to you?

Judith: I don't know ... I haven't really thought about it much. But when I really screw up I can feel my mom hating me. I can feel it in my chest. I cry and want to hide. I feel a weight on my chest and I just ball like a baby. I'm not evil. I just feel really bad at times.

Dr. Phil: What is the most evil thing you have done?

Long pause and tears started to flow:

Judith: I hurt my mom by having sex when I was a sophomore.

Dr. Phil: Did your mom find out?

Judith: No way. I'd never tell her. She would hate me.

Dr. Phil: How did it hurt your mom if she doesn't know?

Judith: I don't know, I just feel evil. You know, dirty and bad.

Dr. Phil: When did this happen, last year or back in high school?

Judith: Last year. I thought I loved him.

What Judith has shown us is that self-talk is usually experienced as a feeling. It is not a logical reaction to our thoughts. We feel the power of the internal dialogue at our core, and because of this it is more powerful. Most of the time we are not really aware of the self-talk. It is intermixed with the nonemotional thoughts of our mind, but self-talk tends to be emotionally charged. Negative self-talk sneaks into our consciousness and plants a negative emotional *mind mine.* Awkward words, but it is like a land mine in your mind. An emotional booby trap that triggers an emotional reaction. It comes from deep inside and most of the time we don't see it coming.

SELF-TALK IS MORE BELIEVABLE

Self-talk is the interpretation of a situation rather than the situation. This interpretation influences our emotions, behaviors and even our physiology. Because self-talk comes from inside, it avoids most of the filters that we learn to use to evaluate our environment. We take the self-talk thought as a fact. A fact with emotional baggage. Sometimes we don't even see the baggage, we combine that with the fact, making it an even bigger fact.

Let me share an example of how dangerous negative self-talk can be. Over a one year period of time I went through three toilet seats at my office. The reason was that Kim would break them. She didn't mean to. It was just the laws of physics. Kim was a very tall woman who weighed over five hundred pounds. What was most remarkable about Kim was not her weight, it was her sense of humor. She was wonderful to be around. She had loads of friends, many since high school. When she came to my office it was because one of her friends was raped and Kim was her support system.

One day, before her friend's session, Kim asked to use the rest room. When she came back she boldly said, "I'm sorry." She handed me a twenty dollar bill. "I cracked the toilet seat. Buy yourself another one on me!"

"Does this happen often?" I asked.

"When money is tight, I can't afford to pee."

This lead to a conversation about her weight. She told me that she had a thyroid problem and had just learned to live with her condition. She was very open about the troubles her size caused her. When I asked how she knew she had a thyroid problem she surprised me with her answer. "My mom told me when I was in

Dogma does not mean the absence of thought, but the end of thought.

Chesterton

sixth grade."

I suggested that she get a complete physical and her thyroid checked.

A few months later, Kim called and asked for an appointment. She told me, "I had my thyroid checked. It's fine. I'm as healthy as a horse, but bigger, and I need to deal with my anger."

"Anger?" I asked.

"I think that's the feeling I'm going through. I'm furious with my mother for telling me that I was 'big boned' and that I had 'a thyroid problem.'"

Kim had given herself permission to eat anything she wanted to because she believed her weight wasn't under her control. When she found out that the self-talk wasn't correct, her personal belief system was changed forever.

The *talk* part of self-talk can often come from others, but because it is heard from within, it is given substantially more power by each of us.

YOU MUST CONTROL YOUR SELF-TALK TO CONTROL YOURSELF

Thoughts that emanate from within are often stimulated by some external event. This makes your self-talk very powerful. So, if for example, your parents have called you stupid for twenty years, I suspect that when you are feeling upset or nervous you call yourself "stupid."

I have met hundreds of intelligent people who verbalize statements like the following:

> I'm blond today!
>
> I've never been any good with numbers.
>
> I can be such an air head!
>
> My brain just doesn't work today.
>
> I have a terrible memory.
>
> I have shit for brains!
>
> I guess I'm hyperactive or something.

If people are willing to verbalize statements like this about themselves, I can only imagine what they are willing to say to themselves in the privacy of their own thoughts.

I have a sign in my den that states, *Question Authority*. I believe that it is important to question what others tell me. I'm not talking about being rude, I'm talking about being inquisitive. I take this belief personally. I also question what I tell myself. Again, not to be rude, but to be inquisitive. Any thought that is worth having is worth questioning. Now don't take this literally. If you question everything, you won't get anything done. You'll sit on the bed in the morning questioning yourself silly.

It is important for us to be honest with ourselves, to question ourselves, to force ourselves to be personally accountable for our beliefs.

This internal dialogue is the starting point of an educated mind. A mind that seeks knowledge. I challenge you to question authority, yours and others. When questioning others who have power over you, I suggest you question carefully and with appropriate respect. If you come off as a jerk, others with power may enjoy squashing you like a bug. I suggest that you calmly ask, "How come?" if you really want to learn. If you show that you are curious about how someone arrives at a decision, most people are comfortable within themselves to tell you what lead them to their choice. If you attack this very same person, they will defend their decision, good or bad, to the bitter end. This will often be to your detriment.

Questioning yourself can also lead to bitter resistance to change. Ask yourself, "How come?" This may lead you to thoughts that you do not like about yourself. But, without questioning yourself you will never have an opportunity to know your own beliefs.

Haim Ginott, Ph.D. was an amazing psychologist who devised a procedure for helping us to deal with conflict. He recommended a formula called XYZ. Like in math, x, y, and z are place holders that need to be filled in with information from somewhere else. It works like this:

When you're dealing with an emotionally charged situation you ask yourself—

When x.
It made me feel y.
I wish I did z.

By filling in the formula you get insight into your own thoughts and belief system. It is important that you keep each part of the formula singular. You need to really think about the most important single answer for x, y, and z.

Let's look at how this works.

Before the XYZ formula:

You're in class and the teacher states, "Class, by next Tuesday you need to read Chapter Seven and the first 39 pages of Chapter Eight. That's 140 pages by next Tuesday."

The class moans and groans. People start to pack up their stuff and scurry out the door. Your head is racing. Your thoughts start to race:

> One hundred and forty pages! I can't believe I have to do 140 pages. Is he nuts? There is no way I can do 140 pages. This is bull. The book is boring. Is this teacher an idiot? One hundred and forty pages! This weekend I have to deal with Robert coming over. One hundred and forty pages and Robert! I won't do it. I don't deserve this. I can't take this any more. Why do I have to deal with all this shit? I can't. I'm never getting this done. If I blow this class I'm screwed. I need this stupid class to graduate. I can't hear how I didn't finish. Mom will drone on forever about how I ruined her life. I can't do this. I don't deserve this! I have to get out of here. My chest is pounding. Screw it all. My head hurts. I'm going to Pat's house. He better have weed. I don't deserve this shit!

After the XYZ formula:

You're in class and the teacher states, "Class, by next Tuesday you need to read Chapter Seven and the first thirty-nine pages of Chapter Eight. That's 140 pages by next Tuesday."

The class moans and groans. People start to pack up their stuff and scurry out the door. Your head is racing. Your thoughts start to race:

> One hundred and forty pages! I can't believe I have to do 140 pages. Is he nuts? What's that stupid formula? Oh yeah, XYZ:

> When x.
> It made me feel y.
> I wish I did z.

<u>When</u> I got the one hundred and forty pages! <u>It made me feel</u> overwhelmed.

<u>I wish</u> I could control my overwhelmed, self-talk bullshit, so I can figure out a way to deal with this.

I can do this, It can't be impossible. Seven days until the next class. Seven goes into 140? I kind of hate math, ... 20 times. Twenty pages a day. I can do 20 pages, even if this book is as boring as watching paint dry.

By using the formula and keeping the problem singular you are able to prevent it from getting out of hand. The hardest part is respecting that you are in control of your own self-talk.

By recognizing—then controlling your own self-talk—you become a powerful force.

Jay tried the XYZ formula but found that it didn't work for him:

Jay: I did the XYZ with the problem with my boss but it didn't work for me.

Dr. Phil: Did you stay focused on one problem at a time?

Jay: I think so.

Dr. Phil: Did you truly question your own thoughts?

Jay: I guess.

Dr. Phil: Teach me what you did.

Jay: I was really pissed with my boss for showing off his power. I really hate it when he treats me like I'm an idiot. Like his slave.

Dr. Phil: Makes sense, what did you do?

Jay: I wanted to quit. I walked off to the bathroom to cool down. I played the XYZ game and it didn't work for me. I didn't figure out the problem.

Dr. Phil: Play it out loud for me. What was x?

Jay: I calmed my thoughts down and said to myself, when Barry treats me like his slave (x). It makes me feel like quitting (y). I wish I could quit (z). But that's the problem. I can't quit 'till the end of the semester. I need the job.

Dr. Phil:	I'm not sure if you really answered the *y* part honestly.
Jay:	Sure I did, I wanted to quit.
Dr. Phil:	Quit? Or get treated with more respect?
Jay:	Barry is a bastard. I really want to come back in five years and show him that I have made it—but he is still the manager of a rat hole restaurant.
Dr. Phil:	Sounds like you want to be done with this part of your life. You're tired of being a poor college student who has to flip burgers.
Jay:	Kind of. I kind of like my job. I wouldn't want to do it for a real job. You know, I can do better.
Dr. Phil:	Is it a fake job?
Jay:	Not fake, just what I have to do to get through school.
Dr. Phil:	Kind of like a stepping stone to your next...
Jay:	Yeah. I don't like the way Barry treats the college students. He is a real prick. Power hungry.
Dr. Phil:	Sounds like your XYZ formula has changed.
Jay:	When Barry treats me like his slave (x). It makes me feel like he enjoys bossing me around (y). I wish I could stay focused on why I need this job (z). It is my stepping stone. I won't be working for Barry forever and I will be moving on.
Dr. Phil:	You sound more powerful.
Jay:	When I'm rich, maybe I'll buy the restaurant just to boss Barry around. (With a big smile) Is it mean to have such thoughts?
Dr. Phil:	When you feel safer—I suspect you won't need to step on others to feel good about yourself.

It takes practice during calm times to think about how to question your own thoughts. Enjoy questioning yourself. It is a form of mental chess that only gets better and more clearer with experience. To run your life you need to control your own self-talk.

SUPERFLUITY

HOLLY:

I have always had a little voice in the back of my head that tried to make sense of things that have happened in my life. I want to talk about something that has stayed with me for my whole life:

> "Self-talk is powerful. It comes from inside
> you. It comes from your past."

I completely agree with Dr. Phil, that we remember the negative better than the positive. I heard my mom on a daily basis ask me if I thought she looked fat in a certain outfit that she was wearing, or if I thought that she looked good in her style. I heard my dad, and later my step dad, tell me that I looked fat, or to lose some weight.

> "A lot of our self-talk is accidentally implanted.
> It is given to us by others we feel are powerful in
> our lives."

This has stayed with me, and even now I still ask my boyfriend if he thinks I look fat, "Are you sure that I don't look fat?" I will ask just to make sure. This is a ridiculous type of self-talk. Instead of having the devil on one shoulder, and the angel on the other shoulder, I have my "Do you think I look fat" fetish. I don't think that I picked this up from my girlfriends growing up. I think that it was instilled in me by my mom, and by the men in my life. This is one Law that I am still working on now, though I know that one day, I will be confident enough that I will not have the "fat fairy" on my shoulder making sure that I don't look large.

Dr. Phil would say to put it in the formula:

When X.
It made me feel Y.
I wish I did Z.

So, here's my formula to why my self-talk is the way it is:

When you asked me if I thought you looked fat. (X)
It made me feel confused as to if I should feel this way too.
(Y)
I wish I could understand why you asked me this. (Z)

After learning this life law I can now put this into perspective. Maybe when my mom was growing up she was called fat on a daily basis. I still need to get through this on my own, no matter what happened to her back then.

Life's Law #5

Control your perceptions

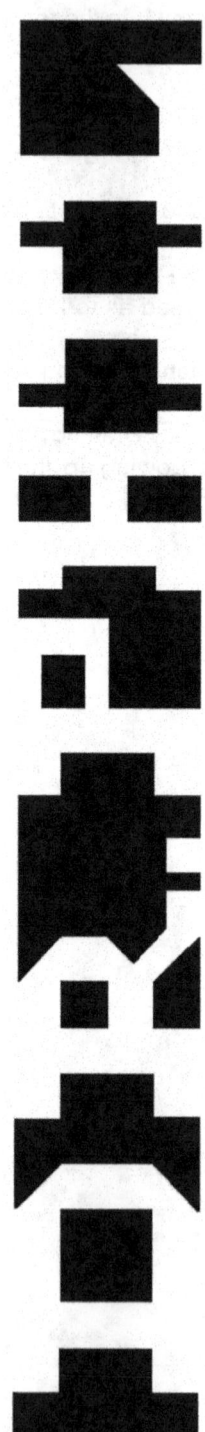

What does this grouping of shapes mean? Hint: It has something to do with your beloved author.

5. LIFE'S LAW #5

Control your perceptions

When I was ten or eleven I went camping with family and friends at a state park in the Adirondack Mountains in upstate New York. On the first day we all went down to a large snow fed swimming hole. The water was very cold and I didn't like the fact that I could not see the bottom. The cold water was constantly being churned by the "buttermilk falls" that rushed down the mountain side into the picturesque pond. This place was beautiful. It had rocks on three sides and was much larger than the public pool I was wading around in back home. I was a very new swimmer, unable to talk myself into even taking the deep end test at the pool. I had a problem. Everyone, including my stupid little brother, was having a ball, swimming to the far side of the swimming hole and jumping off the rocks. But not me. The width of the pond seemed to grow whenever I got five feet from my safe shore.

To add to my fear, fellow campers were all laughing about "How the little fish nibbled at their toes." Everyone thought it was wonderful. I wanted to go back to camp. I didn't say that however. Because, in my family, like most, (unfortunately) if they smell fear they tease you forever.

That first night around the campfire I spent most of my time furious with myself. I was sure that I was the only person who was petrified of swimming to the other side of the swimming hole.

When I was safe in my sleeping bag, I resolved to myself that the next day I was going to swim across the pond *or die trying*.

By the time my slow family got to the swimming hole the morning was mostly spent. The sun was high, and the pond had grown. I steeled myself for the inevitable. I jumped into the frigid water and flailed away with my arms, kicking madly with all my might. My eyes were tightly closed. My heart was pounding. I beat the water with everything I had. I was doing it. I was going to conquer the vast waters.

When I opened my eyes I was overwhelmed with despair. I was only half way. I felt panic take hold. My lungs were burning. My legs were heavy. My fingers refused to move due to the cold. I was gasping for air. I was going to die, and I didn't care.

I was nibbled on. Something had tasted my lower leg. I perked up in the water, peered through the murk to try to see *the cute little fish* that was playing with me. An algae covered basketball with a head bit me. Hard! A huge snapping turtle was going to devour me! I kicked at it, started to flail my arms and I didn't stop until I rammed into the rocks on the far side of the pond. I had made it. My leg was bleeding from a small bite and my hands were cut from smashing into the rocks. All that didn't matter. I was alive. Then I noticed that I had swum across (I didn't even want to think about how I was getting back).

Looking back on that incident, I am amused that I was okay with the idea of drowning, but there was no way I was going to be eaten. Being eaten motivated me, drowning didn't. Perception counts. Reality is much less important.

Our brains do not know the difference between thought and reality. You can see this at any movie theater. Movie goers go through the full range of the emotions that the actors portray on the big screen. People lean to the left if the plane on the screen leans to the left. People feel like they are falling when the camera rushes to the edge of a skyscraper or cliff.

The American Heritage Dictionary defines **perception** as:

> *Psychology* - Recognition and interpretation of sensory stimuli based chiefly on memory.

The "chiefly on memory" part is what I would like to talk to you about. As we go through life we experience our world. This experience is accumulated into understanding. This *understanding* is a guidepost that we compare new experiences against. This comparison is the filter that our mind judges our world by. The process of filtering information through our memories is how we interpret our experiences. Thus, our personal experiences are our reality. Our reality is our perceptions and we make sense out of our world through our perceptions.

This may seem like a bunch of psycho-babble, but it's worth sticking with me on this. If our perceptions are our interpretations of the world, it must mean that how we interpret our world *produces* our reality. To put it simply. There is no reality, only our perception of reality. With this information we have power. We have power over the filters that interpret our reality.

No reality. What a concept! Let's look at this in the real world (sorry about the pun). Scott shows up at work to find a pink slip in his *In Box.* He is being let go. After five years he is unemployed. Is this a good thing, or a bad thing? The answer is neither. It is just a situation. What makes it a good or bad situation is how Scott interprets it. For all we know, Scott has been trying to find the courage to look for a new job. Maybe he was bored with his old job. But, his boss was a great guy and he didn't want to leave with this big project looming over everyone's head. This would make this pink slip a good thing.

However, if Scott recently purchased a new car with a huge monthly payment, this pink slip would be a bad thing. Scott's history filters the news into the *good* or *bad* category. News isn't good or bad, it simply is. We perceive the good or bad of it.

At this point most smart people love to prove me wrong. "What if the reality is bad, like the loss of life or something?"

It depends on how you deal with the tragic loss of life. History is full of terrible things that are forged into good.

A teen died drunk at the wheel of his parents' car. His parents had the car towed to his high school's parking lot. Through their pain they wanted the crumpled car to teach.

A seventeen year young boy dies in a senseless motorcycle accident. His parents donate his heart, kidneys, and corneas so others can live.

Noah did nine years in prison for selling drugs. When I met him he was telling his story so others could learn. He said, "The nine years I spent in prison saved my life. I have no doubt about it. If I had not gone to prison I would have died on the streets of San Francisco from the twenty years of bad choices that I had made." For most of us, nine years in prison would be perceived as bad, but for Noah it was perceived as good.

Stephen Hawkins, the preeminent mathematician and astronomer, was crippled by ALS, Lou Gahrig's Disease. His body is out of his control. His mother was once interviewed and she told how she worried about how he drank and played around in college and how he never applied himself. "If it wasn't for his illness he never would have taken the time to apply his mind." I am sure that Mrs. Hawkins doesn't see her son's disease as a blessing. However, the way he has used his mind to advance our knowledge of the universe is definitely a blessing (and, he got to play himself on an episode of Star Trek).

This morning I awoke and turned on the radio. The newscaster was explaining ... "The hope is that the plane had mechanical problems and the accident was not a terrorist attack." As I learned more about the plane crash in Queens, New York, two months after the World Trade Center and Pentagon terrorist attacks, I too was hoping for accident versus terrorism. It is easier to deal with an accident than a terrorist attack. But either way, 250 people are still dead. This is a powerful example of how one's perception is controllable. If the plane crash had been an accident, we can learn from it. We can make aircraft safer. But, if the crash had been a terrorist attack, we would have been dealing with planned chaos and hatred.

We all choose our own perceptions. We personally assign meaning to our world in an attempt to make sense of it. The process of assigning meaning is the use of personal filters. Our filters are learned through experiences. How you react is a choice.

CAN YOU TRUST WHAT YOU SEE?

In this section I want to show you how
easy it is for our perceptions to be tricked.

In this section I want to show you how
easy it is for our perceptions to be "tricked."

[Do you read using mostly the tops or the bottoms of the letters?]

In this section I want to show you how easy it is for our percep-tions to be "tricked." We humans have five senses: sight, sound, touch, taste, and smell. Each sense can be "tricked." Due to the restraints of this book, I will mainly show illusions having to do with sight (it's really hard to trick the other senses in print).

Some of the illusions I will present will only work the first time. After you have experienced them they will never trick you again. Your mind will have learned more about your world, and you will be able to use this knowledge in the future. One time illusions are still fun. You can show them off to friends.

Some of the illusions that I will present will trick your brain every time. Even though you know the trick, you will have to *figure it out* every time. Chalk it up to being human, or at least an animal. Even though you know that you are being tricked you will not be able to override your perceptions. In fact, this is why I have written this section. It is important to know that you can be easily tricked even when you know there is a trick being presented. In this chapter you are learning how to control and understand your perceptions. Here we look at how our perceptions get tricked. I am using visual perceptions just to prove a point about perceptions in general.

Before we get started looking at vision, let me explain two tactile experiments you can try at home.

WHICH IS THE HEAVIER CAN EXPERIMENT:

What you need are three different size empty food cans, un-cooked rice, and a kitchen scale. In the recycling container I found an 8 (fluid) ounce can, a 16 ounce can , and a 28 ounce can. (The remnants of some awesome slow cooked chili.) Wash and dry each

---

can and watch for sharp edges. Fill each can with rice so that each can, along with its rice, weighs the same; 10 ounces for example. Cover each can's opening with aluminum foil.

Ask someone to pick up each can and tell you which one is the heaviest. Which one is the lightest? People tend to answer that the small can weighs the least and the large can weighs the most. Even when you tell them that each can weighs the same, they will argue. Why? This illusion is due to our expectations. We expect the small can to weigh less and the large can to weigh more. We are prepared for the weight we expect. We judge the weight through our expectations giving us our belief of its actual weight.

In my office I have a realistic looking granite rock made out of plastic. It weighs almost nothing in comparison to what a real fist sized granite rock should weigh. When people pick it up the first time they usually end up lifting it so high that they almost hit themselves in the face with the back of their own hand. Some even drop it because their perceptions are so confused.

I HAVE TO GO TO THE BATHROOM EXPERIMENT:

For this experiment you will need three bowls of water. One bowl filled with hot water, the second filled with cold water and the third filled with room temperature water. Place the room temperature bowl in the middle. (You may wish to go to the bathroom before you do this experiment.)

Place a hand in each of the outside bowls. Let each hand get used to the hot or cold water. This usually takes about one minute. Simultaneously place your hands in the room temperature water. Voila! You have tricked your own perceptions. Your brain gives you two different beliefs about the room temperature water, even though your brain knows the water temperature is neither hot nor cold. Don't worry about tricking your own perceptions. You do it all the time. We all do.

VISUAL ILLUSIONS:

Visual perception is the process of making sense of the reception of *electromagnetic energy* taken in by your eyes. Simply put, your eyes receive light waves the same way your radio receives radio waves or your television receives a television signal through a cable or from the antenna on the roof.

In the following illustrations you will see that your perceptions can be easily confused. Are the lines between the "> <" symbols the same, or are they different lengths?

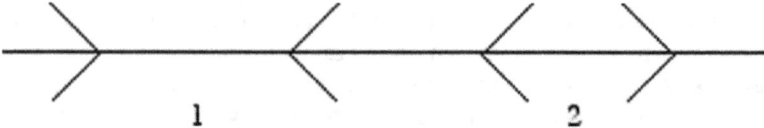

As you can guess, line #1 and line #2 are the same length. But they do not *seem* to be the same length. The angle and direction of the < messes with our ability to determine the length. In the following illusions the lengths are the same, but the angles have been changed. Lines #1-6 are the same size, but they are not perceived to be the same size.

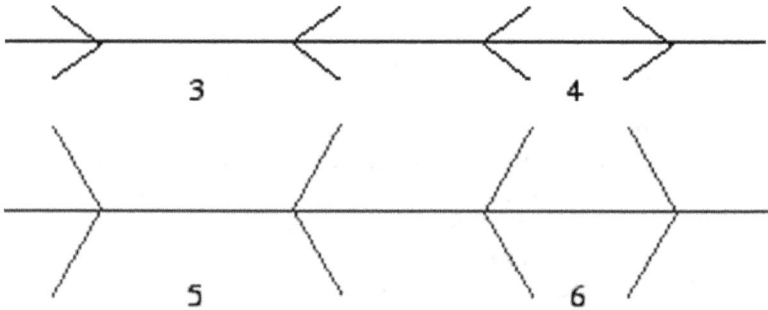

Even things you are used to seeing can be difficult to perceive if shown to you in an unusual manner:

Once you know what the above is, you will probably not be fooled by this same illusion for a long time, if ever. These are the numbers one through seven hidden by a process called *symmetrical camouflage* (Cover the first half of each symbol to see it easier).

In the next illusion the five balls look misaligned. If you check you will find the balls are indeed aligned. Our eyes combine the jittery effect of the lines to make the balls seem out of alignment.

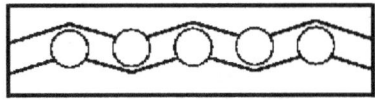

Our eyes can be tricked by misalignments and "jittery" art. The next illusion is called Jittered squares:

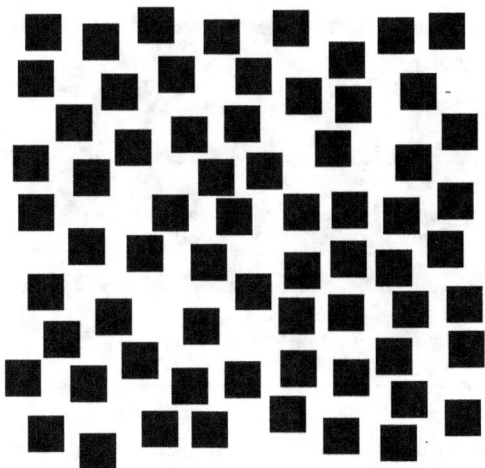

The randomly placed squares look tilted, but they are not. Feel free to use a straight edge to prove to yourself that the above squares are really aligned (this illusion is so powerful that most people have to prove it to themselves).

Illusions are what make movies work. Most people don't spend time thinking about it, but movies don't really move. We just perceive that they do.

How far that little candle throws his beams!
So shines a good deed in a naughty world.

William Shakespeare
The Merchant of Venice

What is a weed? A plant whose virtues have not been discovered.

Ralph Waldo Emerson
Fortune of the Republic

When you watch a movie you are seeing a series of static images run back to back at a high speed. This gives the perception of motion through the process called "persistence of movement." Brothers Louis and Auguste Lumiere demonstrated the first movie in 1895 in Paris. Their demonstration showed a jockey riding a horse. Now we have British kids riding on brooms. Isn't technology wonderful?

Let's take a moment to mess with your tongue. The following is supposed to be the hardest tongue twister in the English language.

Peggy Babcock

Say it ten times fast. Ask friends to do the same so you can enjoy laughing at them.

In the next visual illusion you need to bring the image towards yourself. As you go cross-eyed, the illusion occurs.

Can you get the big fish to eat the small fish?

What do you see?

This illusion was developed by a psychologist named Joseph Jastrow at the start of the 1900's. Is it a rabbit or a duck? This is an example of an ambiguous figure that is influenced by the direction of our focus. If we focus on the left, we tend to see a duck's beak. If we focus on the right, we tend to see a bunny.

In the next figure we see either an Eskimo looking into a cave or the silhouette of a proud Indian face (lots of little boys report seeing a boy peeing on a wall).

Our perceptions can be primed to see something that is not really there. This can be very important in criminal cases that rely on witness testimony to determine guilt or innocence. With the advances in genetic evaluation of criminal evidence we have learned that eyewitness testimony has serious drawbacks. Of the first 32 death penalty cases that were overturned by genetic testing, 28 of them had been convicted on the eyewitness testimony of credible witnesses.

Let's try a little priming illusion just for fun. Ask a friend to quickly repeat the word "white" ten times. When they are done, ask your test subject, "What does a cow drink?" Don't hesitate with your question. Most people answer "milk." But, we know cows drink water! We primed the subject with his knowledge about cows. Most people think of "cows" and "milk" as synonymous.

This section was fun, but I hope I was able to prove to you that your perceptions are personal and prone to inaccuracies. This should lead you to question your own beliefs.

PURIFY YOUR FILTERS

Belief is often confused with fact. Just because you really believe something doesn't make it a fact. A fact is just that—factual. What I mean by this is that a thought that can withstand the test of repeated scrutiny is <u>more likely</u> to be a fact. If a thought is not questioned it is a belief, but not necessarily a fact.

So? You may be asking yourself. This is a big deal? If we hold onto beliefs that we do not scrutinize we are prone to develop inaccurate personal filters. Earlier we met Kim. She was sure she had a biological problem that caused her to be overweight. She did not question this belief. We learned that her belief was inaccurate. A false truth which she had filtered many thoughts through.

If we do not keep track of our beliefs and how they effect us we are being controlled by them.

As we grow and mature we develop filters that we strain our thoughts through. When I was fifteen I would have comfortably told you that I did not like spaghetti. I was sure of it. But when I tried "real" spaghetti, spaghetti with flavor, I instantly changed my belief. My present belief is: I like home made Italian style spaghetti; I dislike canned spaghetti I got from the school cafeteria every Wednesday. If my filter (I hate spaghetti) was rigid I would not have tried real spaghetti. I wouldn't have know what I was missing out on.

Rigid filters are not challenged. This can be good or bad. I have a rigid belief that I really dislike being poked in the eye. I'm comfortable with this belief. But I need to control this positive rigid belief if I need eye surgery. I need to allow the surgeon to poke me in the eye for my own benefit. If we do not keep track of our beliefs and how they affect us we are being controlled by them.

Mr. Sachs was a forty-four year old business man. He seemed physically fit. He prided himself on working hard and playing hard. During a routine insurance medical exam, Mr. Sachs was furious when his doctor wanted to give him further tests. He threw a fit and refused to have the tests that were recommended. "There is nothing wrong with my heart, I'm as fit as a horse."

Two weeks later, Mr. Sachs was taken to the hospital after complaining of chest pains. By the time he got to the hospital he was feeling better and refused treatment. He told them that he was just having heartburn and needed to get home to bed. He had a big meeting in the morning and couldn't miss it. He did agree to come in for tests the following day.

Mrs. Sachs made the appointment for her husband and forced him to go. When Mr. Sachs entered the cardiac test area he was breathing heavily and sweating profusely. He proudly told the cardiac specialist, "I don't need any tests, I'm as healthy as a horse. I just ran up and down the stairs for fifteen minutes." Mr. Sachs had done just that. To prove to his wife that she was over reacting, he had run up and down the hospital stairs.

When I met Mr. Sachs he was weak and listless. "I couldn't believe it," he whispered. "My doctor was right. I had a heart attack as they were putting on the monitoring wires. I think I would have died if I wasn't already in the hospital." Mr. Sachs damaged his heart severely. His rigid belief ("I'm as healthy as a horse") cost him seventy percent of his heart muscle and almost killed him.

You need to know how your filters influence you. Only by knowing this will you be able to use your learned filters correctly. You need to question your self-talk. It seems to be human nature that we do not notice our own short comings. It is difficult to be self-objective.

STAGNANT BELIEFS HOLD YOU IN THE PAST

Many people develop negative filters that are so powerful that I call them **Stagnant Filters**. Stagnant Filters are negative beliefs about yourself that are extremely dangerous.

Mrs. Gorman was seventy years old. She came to my office because she was depressed. She had worked as a waitress for fifty-five years and retired only when her legs would not let her do her job any longer. As I got to know Mrs. Gorman it was interesting that she had one entrenched stagnant belief through which she filtered most of her life through.

Dr. Phil: It sounds like it is very hard for you to live on your social security.

Mrs. Gorman: It is. After my rent and the heat I don't have enough for my medication. I never expected to live this long so I didn't put any money away.

Dr. Phil: Any family?

Mrs. Gorman: I had a sister who died when she was twenty-eight. She had breast cancer you know. It runs in my family.

Dr. Phil: In your family?

Mrs. Gorman: My mother was a saint. She died of breast cancer when I was a little girl. My grandmother died young too, I think it was breast cancer, but no one really kept records back then.

Dr. Phil: How is your health?

Mrs. Gorman: I'm as fit as a fiddle. I'm never sick. A cold every now and then. If it wasn't for my arthritis I'd be just dandy. I never thought I would live this long, with cancer in my family and all.

Dr. Phil: Are your friends helping out?

Mrs. Gorman: To tell you the truth, I'm not a very social person. I saw people at work. I never really had friends.

Dr. Phil: You seem to like people. I don't understand.

Mrs. Gorman: It seems silly when I think about it now. But for years I have avoided making friends. I never married, but I had lots of fellas calling when I was young. It seems silly now ... but I thought I was going to die young. So I never let anyone get too close. I didn't want to hurt them. It's so hard when people you love die, you know. I thought God was going to take me any day.

Dr. Phil: Any day?

Good can imagine Evil; but Evil cannot imagine Good..
W. H. Auden

Mrs. Gorman: It sounds so silly, I know, but I always thought that I was going to die ... in a day or two.

Mrs. Gorman taught me that she had lived her life waiting to wake up ill and find that she would die in a few days like her mother and sister did. Her stagnant belief kept her from making friends outside of her work acquaintances. I got to know Mrs. Gorman quite well over a few months. She was a wonderful lady with charm and grace. Unfortunately, she had been lonely for close to fifty years.

Often stagnant beliefs are imprinted on one's mind very early. Over the years I have heard lots:

· My mother always told me I was going to get fat.

· My father always said I would amount to nothing.

· I've never been good with numbers so I seem to get ripped off all the time.

· My parents liked my sister because she was the smart one.

· I only have bad luck!

· Black people are lazy (racism is a stagnant belief that undermines the individual and the community).

· Indians drink all the time.

· I couldn't learn that at my age.

· There's no one out there for me.

· I've never done that ...

· No one in my family has ever ...

· It's not really stealing, they won't even miss it.

You need to understand your own stagnated beliefs so that you can control their influence over you. Earlier we talked about questioning authority. Within yourself your thoughts are authoritative. You need to question them. Your individual power is controlled by your own perceptions.

SUPERFLUITY

REID:

The part about "stagnant beliefs" describes one of my faults to a tee. Somewhere along the line I convinced myself that I was bad with numbers and was doomed to forever fail math classes. While it is true that math comes to me much more slowly than other subjects, there is no reason I can't succeed in math if I put sufficient effort into it. Another of my stagnant beliefs was that I would always be weak and skinny. For a long time I just accepted that my body type was predetermined by my genes, that I could never vary from that "blueprint" significantly no matter how much I worked at it. Only recently have I decided this was false, and I've been steadily gaining weight (my goal) since I decided to start lifting weights.

———

A few more tongue twisters:

3 times fast: *Soldiers Shoulders*

3 times fast: *Red leather, yellow leather*

A cup of proper coffee in a copper coffee cup.

Sally saw Sylvester stacking silver CD's side by side.

———

6. LIFE'S LAW #6

Life rewards calculated risk

Rebecca was a well spoken, attractive, scared girl of sixteen. "I'm trying to get my shit done, but I'm not good at getting it done!" She exclaimed as she fought off tears. She wanted to storm out of my office, but, she couldn't figure out a way for her hurt feelings to be all my fault.

Dr. Phil: Please try to pick up the tissue box.

Rebecca: What?

Dr. Phil: Please try to pick up the tissue box.

Rebecca: Sure, I guess...

She picked the box up and started to hand it to me.

Dr. Phil: No Rebecca, I asked you to <u>try</u> to pick up the tissue box, not to pick up the tissue box.

She placed it back down on the coffee table. She looked puzzled.

Rebecca: I <u>can</u> pick it up!

Once again she picked up the box.

Dr. Phil: I asked you to <u>try</u> to pick it up, not to pick it up.

Rebecca: Not to?

She pretended to pick up the box. She exaggerated its weight and acted as if she couldn't pick it up.

Dr. Phil: That's it Rebecca, you either do or you don't. There is no try.

Rebecca: But I'm trying to pick it up.

Dr. Phil: You either pick it up or you don't. Try is a word we use to give ourselves a way out when we fail.

Rebecca: Fail! I am trying to get more organized. I really am.

She busted into tears.

Dr. Phil: So—You are either getting more organized or you are staying the same. You have to do something for there to be a change.

Rebecca: It's too hard. There's too much to do.

Dr. Phil: That may be so, but even a little change means that you are doing something.

YOUR BEHAVIOR IS JUDGED NOT BY YOUR INTENTIONS, BUT BY YOUR RESULTS.

I should be a multi-billionaire. That's right, billionaire — with a "B." The reason I should be a billionaire is because I invented the Frisbee when I was four or five years old and picnicking with my family at a park. I took a paper plate off the table and winged it with all my might. It was amazing. It flew! I had just invented the Frisbee. My mother was not impressed with my aeronautical skills and growled at me to stop making a mess. This scared me so much that I ran off whimpering. The newly invented Frisbee was lost in the confusion of my mind. So, if the truth be told, it is my mom's fault that I am not a multi-billionaire. Years later, some guy named, uh, Wham-o I guess, wasn't traumatized by his mother and went on to market a flying disc. He is probably a multi-billionaire.

I think it is a fair assumption that if I happened to meet Mr. Wham-o one day he would not recognize my accomplishments. I suppose he would not share his wealth with me, the true (kind of) inventor. He would probably point out that if I really was the inventor I should have patented my idea. Then I should have developed the plastic molds. I should have figured out the packaging, marketing, and the distribution of my product. I did none of that. I simply whimpered off into the poor house of obscurity.

I once heard an inventor talk about the difficulty of getting a product to market. He said, "The ideas are easy, I have them all the time. The hard part is getting others to back you with cold hard cash so you can bring the ideas to the marketplace."

The same is true in most parts of an individual's life. I have heard it a million times (at least). "I was going to ...." You know what I'm talking about, the Indian tribes: the Shouldas, the Couldas, and the Wouldas. "I should have ..." "I could have ..." "I would have ..." Probably the three leading openings of the excuse sentence.

"The road of life is paved with good intentions."
"I meant to ..."
"I was going to ..."
"I forgot ..."
"I didn't know how to start ..."
"I would have done it but ..."

The list is huge. We love to let ourselves off the hook if we do not accomplish. Excuse making is an international pastime. I am very strict on this subject with myself. Either I did it, or I didn't do it. I am on time, or I am late. No excuses. If I am late, I messed up. It wasn't traffic or anything else. It was my lack of awareness or self understanding. I am responsible for my life. I take this responsibility seriously.

Are you responsible for your life? Do you take your responsibilities seriously?

I am frequently told by parents, "My child doesn't act his age." The key word in this sentence is the word *act*. The root of the word *action*. Life is action. We are judged by our <u>completed</u> actions. You either do or you don't. <u>Do</u> is an action, <u>Didn't Do</u> is an inaction. An inaction is a nothing. You are judged not by your intentions, but by your results. If someone runs into your car, do you care that he intended to stop? I doubt it. You judge the person by his action. (Using your car as a brake!) If your friend told you that she would pay back your loan by the end of the month so you could pay rent, does it help you pay rent if she <u>meant to</u>? We are all judged by our actions.

"What have you done for me lately?" is the real world. If you come home on time sixty seven times in a row, great. When you're late, does anyone really care about your sixty seven wins? Probably not. Would your landlord care that your friend really did mean to pay you back? Or, does the landlord judge you by your actions (You don't pay your rent on time and you loaned his money to some idiot who didn't pay you back).

If a condom works, do you really think about it much? Probably not. You just lie there thinking about how good you are in bed. But, if a condom breaks you are suddenly very attentive. Wow, you're a lot like your parents or your landlord, always focusing on the lack of appropriate action and bitching about it.

WHAT IS CALCULATED RISK?

A calculated risk is a risk that is well thought out and judged to be sound. It is a chance for you to totally screw up or to totally do well. It is not a fifty-fifty chance. That would be gambling. It is a 87.347% chance or a 92.125% chance. It is not a 100% certainty. Sometimes it is a gut feeling. Should you ask that person out? Should you apply for that new job? Should you do something that scares you?

Fear holds most people back from being amazing. Because

> *We are judged by the outcome more than by our behavior*

there is a chance that they will not reach their goals, many people never attempt to reach their goals. And, of course, they never reach their goals.

A problem is an opportunity in work clothes.

Henry J. Kaiser, Jr.

Let's say you want to get to the top of a mountain to see what you can see. You can stay in your safe valley and talk about it, "I'm going to..." or you can start walking up the mountain. Let's say you only take one step. You fall and break your ass. Is it a loss? Definitely not. You are one step closer than you were before. You can only lose by not attempting the trek.

Let's say you work your ass off. Despite attempt after attempt you only get most of the way up the mountain. Did you lose? Definitely not. You see a lot from your new skill level. The only loss would have been not to attempt.

Life is full of examples of people that never started their lives. They never took any calculated risks. They were the same person at nineteen as they were at eighteen. No growth in a whole year. Now that is a loss!

I find that most people learn more from their losses than their victories. For years I have been asking amazing people how they got to where they are in their lives. Inevitably, they talk about learning from their mistakes, picking themselves up and making a better calculated risk the next time. And the next time, and the next time, and the next time.

The loss could be love, money, work—whatever. The reality is that we learn as we go. If you stop learning I feel sorry for you. We learn from activity. We understand ourselves through activity. Without action we are not emotionally alive.

I often meet new adults who are sure that they don't have a chance. They are sure that they are doomed. With that self-talk they are doomed. We know that self-talk needs to be questioned and controlled.

HOW CAN I DO IT DIFFERENTLY?

When life sets up a road block and you fall flat on you face you have to pick yourself up and clean off your wounds (especially the wounds to your pride). Once you're standing again, you have to ask yourself this question, "How can I do it differently?" Your job is to figure out how to calculate the way it can be done. Lots of people try to tell you why they are sure that it can't be done, but only the Smart Stubborn focus on how to do it differently. Your power comes from looking at the problem from lots of different ways until you see a new way to get your needs met. Being a Smart Stubborn is a way to learn as you go. Gaining and reevaluating what you know and learning how to use your accumulated knowledge gives you power. Knowledge is maybe 10% of life. The vast majority of life is action.

The first 10%: Knowledge
You are or you will become what you think about the most.
The second 90%: Action
Without action you have nothing but inaction.
Inaction is nothing.

For example, many people talk about wanting to lose weight. "Come the first of the year, I'm going on a diet." "The day after my birthday, I'm going to eat better." This self-talk is usually all talk with no action. If you really listen to this type of self-talk you really hear, "Not today, it isn't really important to me today. I hope it will be important to me some other day." With positive self-talk you hear yourself saying, " I walk every day. I care about myself and walking is important to me. I am worth taking care of." When self-talk is positive, it builds upon itself.

LIFE REWARDS ACTION

I have heard it put lots of different ways, but the most succinct statement on the subject is *life rewards action*. You have to choose the best action to get to your goals. If you want a good grade in History, choose to put down the Game Jerk controller and throw yourself into studying history. If you want to stop smoking, do it. Stop smoking. Not at the end of this pack or on New Year's. Right now! Stop. Make the words an action. If you want to stop smoking and tell yourself, "On New Year's day I will quit," you are really saying, "I will smoke until New Year's day." Action is more powerful. You need to judge yourself through your actions. You are a smoker. If you want to stop smoking, take the pack of cigarettes and crush them under your foot. Jump up and down on them and then vacuum up the retched mess. Now you are a nonsmoker. Act like a nonsmoker. Don't buy cigarettes. Don't ask for a cigarette. You are your actions.

If you want to get a particular job, calculate what it will take and motivate yourself to get the damn job. If you want to get a particular honey or hunk to notice you for the wonderful individual that you are, figure out a way to get that information imparted to them. Talk is cheap. Responsible action counts!

You also need to measure others by their actions. Their actions are the score card of their life. If actions are long lived they become commitment. I have a dear friend who has taught JuJitsu for forty five years. Forty five years, wow, that's impressive. That's commitment. It tells you something about someone who has done something for forty five years. Even if you don't like JuJitsu it is still impressive that anyone is committed to anything for such a long time. Commitment is the report card of your life. People believe action. I advise you to measure yourself and others by their actions. Are you willing to do what it takes to get the outcome you desire?

YOUR MORALS ARE YOUR COMPASS

I want to take a moment to talk about your morals. Morals are your sense of right and wrong. Above I asked, *are you willing to do what it takes to get the outcome you desire?* Some people read this as "anything" is OK as long as they win. I want to make this clear—I am not advocating anything goes. I am advocating pushing yourself.

John Hinkley wanted to tell Jodie Foster that he loved her, so he attempted to assassinate President Reagan. That is simply wrong. You can't do anything you want. You have to make your choices within the confines of moral behaviors.

Your morals need to be black and white. Right or wrong. I advise that you live your life 100% of the time according to your morals. When you get to that point you will be happy and proud of yourself.

Morals are not gradations. You cannot be 97% moral or 63% moral. You either are or you are not. When evaluating your own behavior, think about whether your actions are responsible and caring.

When I talk about "do what it takes" I am definitely talking about moral calculated risk. Most often it looks like more effort, more self motivation, greater belief in yourself, and actual task completion. It never looks evil.

Morality is an absolute, not a gradation of right and wrong. Make yourself proud!

In our next chapter we will look at how this measurement thing really works, but for now, it is important to focus on the outcome, not the hopeful words. Action is the outcome of thought (calculated risk).

SUPERFLUITY

HOLLY:

I now see calculated risk in my everyday life. After talking to Dr. Phil about this law and finally feeling comfortable with it, and understanding it, I can chance "calculated risks" often, and feel the rewards.

No one would really call me shy. Friends would probably call me loud, but when it comes to being in front of a crowd, or giving an oral report in front of a classroom full of students, I would go into my shell as if I was a turtle hiding out. To me, being able to do this is a calculated risk. I do want the "A" on my report card, and in order to get what I want I have to get up in front of the class and give my insights on a certain piece that we read. This is a terrifying venture for me, loud yet shy Holly. I know what I want though, and I have to take this calculated risk, no questions asked. I could either not do it, and risk not getting that "A" that I want so badly, or I can stand up there with a face as red as a screaming baby and put my tooth to the grindstone. If this is what it takes, then count me in.

The morning my mom asked me if my step dad had ever done anything to me to make me hate him so much, I could have answered in two ways. Either lie to her and tell her nothing had ever happened, or tell her the truth about him touching me in ways that were inappropriate. Now let's look at this again, I could have either cowered and gone back into my shell, suffering everyday with what happened to me, live my life until the day I turned eighteen years old and left, probably never speaking to my family again, remembering all of the bad times. Or, I could have answered truthfully, and risked my mom, my whole family for that matter, not believing a word that I said and turning on me. This I can say was the biggest calculated risk that I took in my 17 years of life. I told her the truth, and even after all was said and done my (ex) step dad walked away free, and was found not guilty, I took that risk and can say now that my family and I are happier than we have ever been. This was my reward.

I am all for calculated risks, big or small, if there is something that you are afraid of doing, DO IT! No matter if it is telling your mom that big brother beats you up everyday for your lunch money, or if it is running in a marathon, or quitting smoking, OR ANYTHING. I don't want to sound lame or like an overplayed commercial, but just do it!

REID:

I spent a lot of time thinking about this one after I read it. Inaction is something I struggle with on a daily basis. For one thing, I am positively terrified of failure. Far too often this means that I don't take risks. When you have a lot to gain and little to lose, it only makes sense to go for it. My girlfriend, wonderful as she is, is perpetually stuck in her "comfort zone." One result of this is that she eats like an eight-year-old, never straying from a long-established (and very short) list of edible foods. I'll ask her, "Why don't you try this (fill in delicacy)?" She inevitably responds, "No thanks, I don't think I would like that." "How do you know you won't like it if you won't even try it?" I'll press. "I just *know*," she insists. Of course there is risk in trying a new food; you could, quite possibly, dislike it. But if you weigh that possibility with the chance that you might discover your new favorite food, the risk seems acceptable.

7. Life's Law #7

Adapt or stagnate

"Oh Sid, you've gotta stop takin' yourself so lightly!"

7. LIFE'S LAW #7

Adapt or stagnate

At the end of the last chapter I asked you: *Are you willing to do what it takes to get the outcome you desire?* Life's Law #7 is about follow through and how to make shit happen. There are three major problems with follow through.

First, is our own self-talk and how we get in our own way. Second, is the influence friends and family have upon us. And third, is how human nature towards inactivity gets in our way. We will cover the first two problems in this chapter and focus on the third problem in Chapter #8 - Controlling Time.

ARE YOU WILLING TO DO WHAT IT TAKES TO GET THE OUTCOME YOU DESIRE?

I would like to start off with a big fat warning. *The above doesn't mean: Are you willing to do whatever it takes to get the outcome you desire at any cost? Screw everyone else!* I am not advocating that you can do anything just because you want something. That's stupid. I'm stating that you are responsible for your actions and better use heaps of forethought before you initiate a plan. I once received a fortune cookie that read: "A bad person is a good example of a bad example." At the onset of this chapter you must understand that morals concerning right and wrong must be incorporated into *doing whatever it takes.*

A perfect example of this bad example was in today's paper. The lead article of the local section was titled: *Suspect - Shooting was an accident.* The subtitle read: *Redding teen pleads innocent to charges from robbery attempt.*

As in other sections of this book, I will change the name. The article was about 18 year-old Albert Whole; A. Whole for short. It was explained in the paper that A. Whole "...told police he didn't mean to shoot a gas station clerk during a robbery attempt."

A. Whole's sister was quoted, "He's a good kid. He made bad choices."

The article continued:

> The shooting at the Grease Street gas station came four days after A. Whole's friends allegedly burglarized a Shasta Lake home on Thanksgiving Day, stealing as many as 10 guns, A. Whole told police.
> A group of four friends—including A. Whole—

had talked about robbing a bank sometime in the next year, he told police. They spoke of using automatic weapons, grenades and rocket launchers, he said.

But, A. Whole decided to rob the gas station on his own he said, because he owed money to probation officials and didn't want to go back to prison.

So, A. Whole said he waited outside the station for two hours to see if the clerk would leave his booth. About 3:30 AM, he finally threw a rock at a parked car to get the attendant's attention, reports said.

The clerk emerged, and A. Whole appeared with a gun and demanded money, he said. The attendant refused, and the gun accidently went off, the suspect said.

The gas station attendant suffered serious injuries.

In the above story, A. Whole worked it out in his mind that this was a good choice. He didn't think about right and wrong. He didn't think about the gas station attendant. He stayed focused on his problem and gave himself permission to disregard everyone else's needs. This selfish lack of insight is often confused with freedom, but in actuality it is simply stupidity.

WE NEED TO QUESTION OURSELVES

As we take on adulthood we need to constantly question our own authority. We need to look at the bigger picture of our lives.

A few good self-questions are:

Would I be proud of this behavior if it was explained on the front page of the newspaper?

Would I feel right if I had to explain my behavior to _____? (fill in the name of someone you truly respect and would not want to embarrass yourself in front of).

Would I want someone to do this to me, or someone I love?

Would I do this if I knew I was going to be caught?

These self governing moral questions help us make good decisions, even when we want to do whatever initially crossed our minds.

CONFIDE IN YOURSELF AND CHOOSE
YOUR COUNSEL WELL

Often when we want to change something in our world we bounce the emerging idea off others. This sounding board notion is both good and dangerous. It is good to seek out counsel and listen carefully to competent advice. It makes sense to talk to a highly experienced plumber if you are thinking about going into the plumbing trade. It makes sense to learn as much as possible about a school before you choose to apply. But, when you gather information you need to be aware that the giver of the information is filtering her answers through her own life experiences. You need to judge the filters of others.

I once told my Uncle Joe that I was thinking of applying for a doctoral program in psychology on the other side of the country. His words were very specific. "Listen to me boy, you're a poor kid from Rottenchester, how are you getting into grad school?" He continued to explain that school was great for rich kids who buy a fancy piece of paper. He was positive that "people like us" had to make money with our hands.

I have often thought about Uncle Joe's advice. If I had not understood his filters I would probably be a business man in Rochester, New York. There is nothing wrong with that, but it wouldn't have been my choice. I wanted to be a shrink.

Gathering information is imperative to making good choices. Over the years I have found books to be very helpful in giving me solid information. I am very choosy however. I tend not to believe any author who is trying to sell me something other than the information. Be super careful with diet books, make-money-quick books and books that tell you that they know what God is thinking.

ADAPT OR STAGNATE

You need to scare yourself a little bit on a regular basis. If you are not nervous every now and then, you are sitting comfortably inside your safety zone. That may be safe, but it is not living. As we talked about in the last chapter, life rewards action. You have to be doing or you are stagnant. Cesspools are stagnant and like cesspools, people begin to stink up the place when they stagnate.

The best question I know to stop stagnation is: How can I do it differently? How can I do it differently? How can I do it differently? How can I do it differently? How can I do it differently? How can I do it differently? How can I do it differently? How can I do it differently? How can I do it differently? How can I do it differently? How can I do it differently? How can I do it differently?

The preceding is not a typo. You need to ask yourself, "How can I do it differently?" Over and over, until you have lots of choices to work with. With lots of choices you have the best chance to have a great choice in front of you. If you have only one or two choices you may not have any really good choices on your plate. The great choice may not show up until you have challenged your mind 47 times (or some such number). With 47 options to muddle through you have real comparisons. You have stuff to appraise so that you can calculate your risks.

Melissa is ill with cancer. She has three children in their teens. She told me, "It really makes me angry when people say, 'You're so strong, taking care of your kids when you have cancer.' What am I supposed to do, sit around and wait to die? I do what I have to do. I take care of my family."

Melissa is a caring individual who takes pride in her life choices. She has taught me that she is stuck with cancer, but she isn't stuck without choices. She asks herself regularly, "How can I do it differently?" on a little task that you and I take for granted. Melissa is in control of her life.

A homework assignment:

On a piece of paper, a full sheet, write the first letter of your name. Now ask yourself the question, "How can I do it differently?" and draw that same letter differently. Then ask yourself the question, "How can I do it differently?" Ask it again, and again. Fill the page with different letters (for you computer types you may notice that you are changing fonts). Same letter but a different outcome each time

At twenty years of age, the will reigns; at thirty, the wit; and at forty, the judgment.

Benjamin Franklin

I suspect that with each new font you will find it getting harder and harder. At letter number 25 you are probably forging new ground and taxing your mind. Attempt number 30 would not have occurred without the 29 before it. This is an example of how to expand your mind to find a new way to do something you already know.

ONE CHOICE AT A TIME

If you choose to go to the movies you are actually choosing not to do an infinite amount of other things you could be doing instead of going to the movies. By choosing to go to the movies you are choosing not to feed the homeless, not to go for coffee, not to do your philosophy homework, not to ... you fill in the blank. Usually, you can only make one choice at a time. But, often one choice has a ripple effect on numerous other choices. A. Whole chose to rob a gas station which led him to jail. I think that most people his age chose to sleep at 3 AM. This probably wasn't seen as much of a choice. But if A. Whole had chosen to go to bed that fateful night, he wouldn't have chosen to shoot an innocent man.

MOST PEOPLE AND WATER TAKE THE PATH OF LEAST RESISTANCE

Water takes the path of least resistance. It slowly erodes the ground and over time creates a rut. Add more time and water and it forms a stream. After enough time and enough water you end up with a wondrous tourist destination—the Grand Canyon. As we spoke of before, lots of small choices lead to accomplishments. The Grand Canyon was formed from rain drops and commitment to a path.

We humans are going to do something. We are like the rain drops. We are going to be. If we take our little choices and combine them, we become a force. Unlike a river, we are not stuck following the path of least resistance. We can take calculated risks and focus our life force towards a planned goal. If you don't know where you're going—you're there. You're stagnant. If you can adapt, you have a future.

In our next chapter we are going to look at the third major problem of follow-through, controlling time. If we understand how to take advantage of time, we can build destinations.

SUPERFLUITY

HOLLY:

I am so thankful to have learned this Life Law. I would still be like a lot of people I know, totally sucked into drugs and hiding from the reality of life. I have been there, and I know that it is hard as hell to get your head out of the clouds, thinking that life was always meant to be that good. In reality, all you end up with is a wrinkled face, missing teeth, and a dependence that takes over your entire life. This dependence will make you do a lot of things that you wouldn't normally do.

For a long time I was sucked into drugs and I made terrible decisions. I hate to admit it, but I loved doing drugs, it was great, my group of friends and I were like a family. None of us cared about anything, not work, not our "real" families, we were totally sucked into something that was not real. If it was Crystal Meth or pills, we didn't care; all we knew is that we had to have it. Overnight my life became full of friends, parties and drugs; a life that I never wanted to live but was having so much fun in. I never cared when my mom would call, I actually dreaded talking to her because all that she would rave about is how disappointed she was in me. I didn't care, I would talk to her, and then just want to get more spun, or more whatever, and that is what I started to blame everything on. My past, my present, poor Holly, let's go get spun. So we did, for a while.

Then one day I guess I woke up. I was doing terrible in college, I almost got fired from a job that I had had for almost two years, and my family couldn't stand me. I was going nowhere fast, and loving every minute of it, until that one day. I started looking at the future. I started asking myself if I really wanted what I had. Fake friends, no family that I could talk to without feeling judged, no aspirations, nothing. I was nothing. I couldn't understand why it was so hard to give all of that up. I had my own place, why couldn't I just slam the door on all of it and start living again? It took me forever to answer this question. Dr. Phil helped a lot, though I wasn't really interested in what he had to say, he was totally right. I was hiding from reality; I was hiding from my past; I was hiding from all of the pain and anger that I still had to go through; I was drowning all of these emotions with drugs, and stagnating. I took a step out of myself for a bit and realized that this was so right, either I could stay where I was, or I could move on and get through all of these things that I still needed to get through. I chose to slam the door on all that I thought was a reality and began to move on.

And obviously, that is what I did. Now I can talk about it and write about it. I've adapted, and didn't stagnate, and it was the best thing for me.

8. Life's Law #8

Controlling time

"You're getting sleepy ... you're getting very sleepy..."

8. LIFE'S LAW #8

Controlling time

In Life Law #7, Adapt or Stagnate, we looked at two of the three major problems with human follow through. First, was our own self-talk and how we get in our own way. Second, was the influence friends and family have on us. This brings us to the third major problem: how our nature towards inactivity and distractibility gets in our way. Simply put, how we manage (or probably misman-age) our time.

For many, the word *manage* denotes following rules and being controlled. For countless young adults *being managed* is being told what to do. That sucks! Who wants to be told what to do? I would like to look at this differently.

The word manage means: *To direct or control the use of.* In this chapter we are going to focus on *self* direct and *self* control. We are going to learn how to control time and use it, versus being controlled by it and subservient to it.

British academic and writer, C.S. Lewis wrote,

> The Future is something which everyone reaches at a rate of sixty minutes an hour, whatever he does, whoever he is.

This may seem like a basic truism, but most people lie to themselves about this fact. Let's separate fact from bullshit.

The Fact: We calculate time on planet Earth based on our planet's rotation. One day equals 24 hours. One hour equals sixty minutes. One minute equals sixty seconds. If you do the math, there are 86,400 seconds in a day. Everyday. No more, no less. Everyone gets the same amount. 86,400 little parts of every single day [60 seconds X 60 minutes X 24 hours/day= 86,400].

But: Some people get a lot more done in 86,400 seconds than other people get done.

Why: After reading this far into this book you know the reason, choice. Most people choose to waste time and they do it by not paying attention to their lives or by lying to themselves. You are way beyond most people; you're learning how to control your life to get your needs met. Let's look at how we lie to ourselves.

TIME LIES

There are three major lies we use to trick ourselves concerning time.

1. There is more time in the future.
2. I don't care about time.
3. You can "save time."

1. THERE IS MORE TIME IN THE FUTURE.

Ever find yourself saying, "I'll do it later"? This assumes that later has more time in it than now. Somehow, in your future you have this large chunk of time sitting around waiting for you to catch up to it and use it. My friend Snyder often jokes, "I'll do it in my spare time or my extra time." She is joking about the fact that there is no "extra time" or "spare time." There are only 86,400 seconds in our day. You can't save it up for later. You can't buy more from a clock shop. You can't find more under the bed or in the pocket of an old pair of jeans (which are probably under your bed).

It is important to know that you have only so much time. Time may be infinite, but you are not. You may live 80 years, which is a lot in comparison to the average house fly. But, 80 years is pretty much nothing in the existence of a small class M planet circling around a nothing small yellow star in the dull outer corner of the cosmos. Your life goes by with or without you paying attention.

2. I DON'T CARE ABOUT TIME.

Recently, my fourteen year old son announced, "I'm bored, there's nothing to do!" I did my dad thing and asked, "What do you want to do?" "I dunno, everything is boring." He said as he flopped hopelessly onto the couch. "I know," he continued. "Life can't be boring, only people can be boring." He knows me so well. He used my line before I got to. But, life can't be boring, it just is. What you do with life is what makes it boring or exciting. So, if someone is bored, I'm sure they are boring. They need to do something.

If you are unconscious about time it simply ticks away. It doesn't give a rat's ass about anything. It just is. What makes time valuable is what you do with it.

In our society we punish criminals by making them "waste"

I believe the twenty-four hour day is here to stay.
Max Beerbohm

time. We put them in jail. We give them boredom as a punishment. I often see people who place themselves in self-imposed jails of thought in which their life goes by with little self awareness or personal growth. What a waste. Personally, during the big dirt nap I'll waste all the time I could ever wish to waste. While I'm alive, I want to live.

3. YOU CAN "SAVE TIME."

You can't take a jar of time and put it on a shelf for a later date. Everyday you get your allotment of 86,400 seconds. What you do with it is your choice. Use it wisely or not, at the end of 86,400 seconds the day is over and you're onto your next allotment. What most people mean when they say "saving time" is that they want to do something in less time, leaving more time to do something else.

I find myself trying to "sleep fast" so I can get onto my next set of 86,400 seconds. I don't want to use a lot of seconds sleeping, even though I know that without quality sleep, my awake time is less fulfilling.

I want to drive the shortest way most of the time, so I have time to do something else with the time "saved" from driving the long way. All this word play really means is that I want to get the most done in the shortest amount of time so I can still do more. What we are talking about is efficiency.

The word *efficient* comes from the old English word, *dhe* which means "do." So for a really long time, humans have known that you have to _do_ to get anything done (your ancestors were brilliant). Once you understand that you need to _do_, then the real problem is _how_. What are the ways to do things more efficiently? This will be discussed later, but first let's focus on what to avoid; how to protect ourselves from the dreaded Time Bandits.

TIME BANDITS

Time Bandits is not just a cool English flick from 1981. Time Bandits are things in our lives that rob us of time. Time crooks! The opposite of wasting time is using time efficiently. This big question is really two questions. What to do and what not to do? To answer this we have to look at the negative side of this equation—what not to do. What do we need to avoid, in order to get our stuff done. This time stuff can give you a headache.

The key things to avoid:

ATTITUDE

We have spent a lot of time covering the subject of attitude and how it influences what you do. In fact, I believe it is attitude that holds most people back and makes most people unhappy and unfulfilled. When it comes to time and attitude I want to tell you a story.

Dale is a smart kid who ended up at my office after earning straight 'C's' in his junior year of high school. His parents were not happy that he wasn't trying, and constantly bombarded Dale with the old tired line, "You have so much potential."

When I met with Dale he explained, "I hate homework ... it's boring and useless. It takes too much time for no real reward."

To get his parents off his ass, Dale agreed that he would commit 1 1/2 hours to homework on school nights as long as his parents didn't hover over him or talk to him about "his potential." His parents also agreed.

I met with the family a week later and Dale was very upset with the agreement he had made with his parents. Everyone was honoring their part of the agreement, but Dale was pissed that he wasn't able to get his homework done in 1 1/2 hours. He was very upset that his school was giving him so much "lame" homework.

I suggested that Dale videotape himself doing his homework. My plan was for Dale to do his homework for 1 hour and to spend the next half hour viewing the video to see how much time he was wasting and not really doing his homework. It is my contention that lots of time is wasted during homework periods that people don't realize they are wasting.

The next week the family and I came together and Dale was happy to inform me that he didn't watch any of the tapes.

Dr. Phil: How come, I thought you agreed to watch the tape?

Dale: I didn't have to, I was done in under an hour. I guess I had less homework this week than last week.

Dr. Phil: I wouldn't think so. I've had lots of kids video their homework and they all bounce on in here the next week with a shit kissing grin and say, "Dr. Phil, I didn't have to watch the video." I think they like throwing it back in my face.

Dale: Yeah, kind of I guess, but I didn't have to. I was done.

Dr. Phil: Great, but why were you done?

Dale: I told you. I think I must'a got less homework this week.

Dr. Phil: Could it be you pressed the tape button and sat right down and did your work. No screwing around? No phone calls? No looking for stuff?

Dale: (mouth open) I guess.

We all get in our own way. What Dale experienced was that if he simply started and got it done, the task seemed to be smaller. He didn't have to carry his own attitude around during the "fighting doing homework process." Less attitude weight, less work.

I once met a cool old farmer who made millions in the cow business. He was a whiz with numbers and always good for a dirty joke or two (hundred). He told me that the hard part of being a rancher for him was getting up at 4:45 AM. I asked him how he pulled himself out of bed so early every morning. He said, "My pappy used to tell me, 'Pretend it's something you want to do.'" Attitude counts, even at 4:45 AM.

YOU'RE TIRED

It's hard to get stuff done when you're tired. I joked earlier about "sleeping fast", but it can't be done. Your brain has to clean itself and do daily maintenance or you lose skills. You cannot be efficient when you're tired. A lot of research has been focused on sleep. If you think about it, the Armed Forces would love to have a soldier who didn't need sleep. The research shows that we lose mental acuity when we are tired. If you go without sleep it is not safe. Tired people get injured. Tired people make mistakes.

No one likes to hear this, but pulling all-nighters is a terrible way to study. Research shows that little is retained in the student's long term memory and anxiety is significantly increased.

Respect yourself, make quality sleep a priority.

LACK OF FOCUS

It seems very simple to most patients in my office that you need to make a choice before you can do something. I am often told, "I have so much to do that I can't get anything accomplished."

Time is a great teacher, but unfortunately it kills all its pupils.

Hector Berlioz

Zoe had just turned twenty-six and was working in her first professional job at a midsize law firm. She was feeling the pressure of work when her boyfriend of five years dropped a bombshell on her. He was planning on taking a job four hours away and would only be able to see her on weekends. Her boss, a supportive and caring man, advised her to come and see me when she yelled at the copy machine and scared the office staff.

Zoe: I am being pulled in a million directions. I can't seem to get anything done.

Dr. Phil: What counts most to you?

Zoe: I don't care about any of it, it's all just shit to me!

Dr. Phil: Then why are you bothered?

Zoe: Aren't you listening. I'm going crazy!

Dr. Phil: I doubt it. But you are being emotionally pulled apart. What do you want to do?

Zoe: I don't have any idea (She stared sadly at her shoes).

Dr. Phil: If you don't know what you want to do, you're doing it. Nothing. You've become ineffectual.

Zoe: Can you fix me?

Dr. Phil: You're not broken, you need to focus on what really counts to you. <u>One thing at a time</u>.

Zoe: I can't do that ... I'm swamped at work and I think my boyfriend is dumping me. I don't blame him. I want to dump me too (she half smiled)!

Dr. Phil: I'm not advocating for you to do one thing at a time all day or all week. I want you to focus on one thing at a time throughout your day. When you're at work, focus on the one project that needs your attention the most. When you're at home, focus on the one thing that needs the most attention.

Without focus, Zoe was getting nothing done in any part of her life. When she was at work, she was thinking about home. When she was driving, she was thinking law. When she was with her boyfriend, she was feeling work stress. It's like the old question: How do you eat an elephant? The answer: One bite at a time. If the bite is too big and it is choking you, you need to spit it out and cut it into smaller bites. You can eat an elephant one bite at a time. And, you can accomplish even difficult tasks one bite at a time. However, even at one bite at a time, you need to focus on what you are doing.

I have listed some of the more common reasons that people choke on their responsibilities. Each tends to give talented people lots of difficulty. By keeping these problem areas in mind, and by cutting them into smaller pieces, you will be able to accomplish your desired goals.

UNDEFINED GOALS

You have to be able to define a task to accomplish it. Force yourself to develop a specific definition of what it is you need to get done. It is easy to be pulled off course if you do not clearly see where you are heading.

Leroy told me that he wanted to pick up extra work doing odd jobs in his neighborhood. I asked him what he would put on a big billboard if he could afford a billboard. After a few minutes he said, "I want to make money!"

Leroy was focusing on his need, he wanted money. But, that wasn't going to get someone in the neighborhood to hire him to clean out their gutters. Leroy's problem was that he wanted to make money (a really big bite). He had to spit this problem out and cut it into smaller stuff. With a little practice he came up with the following list which he made into a flyer (Leroy's charm came through in his flyer and in person).

Honest hard working high school senior
looking for honest hard work

My mom has allowed me lots of experience:

Washing windows
Scrubbing floors, toilets and driveways
Moving furniture and cleaning carpets
Painting inside and out

Dependable

On his handouts he listed his mother as a reference and asked prospective customers to call his mother to confirm his skills.

Leroy made $1800 dollars and was later hired by a neighbor to work the counter at his dry cleaning business. He worked there for the two years he went to junior college.

You need to define your goals so that you can make sure you

are focusing on what you value. For example, when I was twenty I worked at McDonald's. It afforded me income with a flexible schedule. I showed up on time and I did what was asked of me. Most of the time I enjoyed my experience, especially when we were busy. Time seemed to whiz by when we were busy.

I knew that I was not planning to learn how to manage a McDonald's and make it my career. For me, McDonald's was not a career move, it was a stepping stone to help me work my way through college. I also learned a lot. To this day I am impressed with how McDonald's is able to make a few pennies profit per customer add up to billions of dollars of corporate earnings.

I recall getting teased by friends for working at McDonald's. But, as I saw it, I had an honest job that worked into my ever changing class schedule. My focus was on getting good grades. I was not concerned that I didn't have the most glamorous job.

Once I was assigned to write a paper on how to do something. The English professor wanted a paper that was so clearly written that an average person could do the task just by reading the paper. I wrote about how to make 64 Big Macs at one time. On busy nights, or when a school team bus pulled in, I would whip out 64 Big Macs in minutes.

McDonald's and that English assignment have served me numerous times over the years. I have often been paid for writing a "how to" article. *How to talk to your teen about sex. How to defuse anger in the work place.* And, I often need to whip out six burgers or four omelets or a shit load of ribs at home.

It is important to keep focused on your goals and creatively adjust to get your short and long term needs met.

DISTRACTIBILITY

Jan consulted with me because she was sure she was not ready for her new promotion. Jan, at age twenty-four, had just found out that she was the new Promotions Director for a mid size radio station. She had all the necessary skills and her goal was to capture this job before her twenty-fifth birthday. However, when it happened, she found herself not sleeping.

Jan's concern was that she was unable to keep track of all her business responsibilities. She reported that she spent half her time looking for papers, contracts, or her glasses. After we talked for a bit it was obvious to me that Jan was highly motivated and incredibly skilled. Her biggest problem was that she was easily distracted. Once Jan mastered the following issues, she shined in her new position.

Clutter: Your work space has to be organized. By keeping necessary things within hand's reach and everything else out of the way, you can help yourself focus. Knickknacks and candy dishes draw your attention away from the task at hand. Most people find that order helps job completion.

Phone: The phone is a tool. Just because it rings, doesn't mean it needs to be answered. Don't let the phone control you. A 30 second phone call can take you off task for a few minutes. It is usually best to stop phone interruptions when you need to focus your mind on a task for a chunk of time.

Interruptions: Control your environment. If your work area is an open door to the world, people will interrupt you and you will be constantly distracted. Protect your space. Control your space (be polite). I was impressed to learn that scary writer, Stephen King, found that his little laundry room with a rickety little school desk worked just fine for him. He liked being tucked off in an obscure place, away from distractions.

You need to control your environment so that you are not distracted. Find what works for you. I did most of my graduate dissertation in the middle of the night at a dumpy restaurant. I found the restaurant noise and the bad coffee helped me block out the world.

Don't get caught up in the look of your quiet space, your control over it is what is important. If you need total quiet, make your work space quiet. If you need lots of light, sun up the place. Respect your needs—then get focused on task completion.

FAILURE TO PLAN

Pearl (16) told me why she got her final history paper in late.

> It was like the whole world was against me. I had only six hours before my paper was due and everything went wrong. I even skipped school to work on it. I couldn't find all my reference notes so I had to go on-line and get them again. That took an hour. My brother used up all the printer ink and I had to go the to store. The traffic was horrible. I couldn't believe it. It cost thirty dollars! I was so pissed. I had to go to my mom's work and get money. She was pissed that I skipped school. She just doesn't understand that I had to skip school

so that I could get the damn paper in by the end of school.

I finally got the stupid paper done and I couldn't get the computer to talk to the printer. I just wanted to throw the thing against the wall. It turned out to be the cord thing. I got the thing printed, but I didn't have a folder to put it in. So I had to go back to the store. When I got the whole thing put together, I wanted to glue a picture onto the front cover. I couldn't find any glue in the whole house. I had to go back to the damn store. Three times I had to fight with traffic.

When I finally got it all put together it looked great. I couldn't believe it when my brother came home. School was over. I turned it in the next day and Mr. Johnson didn't even want to believe that I really tried. The best grade I can get on it now is only a 'B'.

Pearl is not unique. I hear this type of story all the time. If you don't plan, you are doomed. A little planning saves a lot of frustration. This will be discussed further when we discuss personal organization skills.

PROCRASTINATION

I bet that procrastination is the most common way people hold themselves back. The word comes from the Latin roots for *toward tomorrow*. The problem is that when we procrastinate, tomorrow leads to the next day, which leads to the next day. Days become weeks and before you know it, life passes you by.

Procrastination means: *To put off doing something, especially out of habitual carelessness or laziness.* Put simply, procrastination is *a choice.*

A Chinese proverb says, *The best time to plant a tree was twenty years ago. The second best time is now.* It may be an old Chinese saying, but it still works for today. A new American saying could be, *The best time to buy milk is before you need it.* Not as classy but accurate. So, the next time you're feeling pressure over your stuff ask yourself, "Wouldn't it have felt good to have had this stuff done yesterday?"

Over the years I have asked lots of people about their procrastination. What I learned is that most people put off stuff they don't like. Wow! We don't want to start what we don't like. Yep. We avoid discomfort. This was discussed earlier when I advocated for you to leave your comfort zone to create the life you want. You have to confront little discomforts to defeat procrastination.

I have a few suggestions about how to kick procrastination's ass. First, recognize it. You have to be aware of your tendency towards procrastination to realize that it is controlling you. Once you notice procrastination's retched breath, you will find the following head games helpful:

Do the worst first: When you have tasks that you must do but don't want to, do the worst task first. This makes the process feel easier. It's very hard to keep going if the job gets even worse. It is easier to stay motivated if the job gets a little better. Remember, your perception counts.

Make a game out of it: Find a way to put some fun into the crappy job. Set up a way to play with yourself (hey, clean your mind up and stick with me here!). Time yourself, attack the job sideways, add music. Be creative. Laugh in the face of despair. Joke with the toilet as you clean it. Humor helps us to get through many a shitty task.

For a lot of people, setting a deadline for themselves is a game that brings rewards. "I'll get this done by 4:15 if it kills me!" It is self-talk that is motivating.

Add a reward: Pat yourself on the back for your hard work. If it's a beautiful day and you can't stand that you're stuck inside, reward yourself with a walk around the block after you get half your work done. I know a business tycoon who rewards himself with five minutes of shooting hoops after he completes an undesirable task. Keep the reward simple and low calorie. If you get a candy bar after each undesirable task, you will be five hundred pounds in no time. I find that physical activity works well for most people. Walk, hoops, or juggle to help relieve life's tensions. Again, be creative.

Start: Lots of people spend so much time getting ready to start that the project doubles. If Stephen King can make millions of dollars writing in his laundry room, you should be able to kick ass with your cool stuff. I once watched my sister prepare all afternoon for a date that took two and a half hours. Four hours of prep for two and a half hours of date. Life's too short. It's like taking off a band-aid, just rip the damn thing off, feel the pain for a moment, then go on with your life. Slowly peeling a band-aid off lets you feel it for minutes versus seconds. As the sneaker ads tell ya: *Just Do It!*

You can never finish a task if you don't ever start. Life rewards action. You have to complete a task to reap rewards.

Total Void: There are areas in our daily lives where we can become totally void of thought. In these Total Void zones we will find ourselves staring off into the ether with little sign of life registering on our faces. When this occurs it is easy to have thirty minutes quickly turn into three hours. In Total Void our mind is being occupied by random thoughts of nothing. Like a black hole in outer space, the Total Void takes thought into it and never lets it escape. It warps time and space while sucking the life out of its victims. No light can escape a black hole, and no time can be retrieved from a Total Void.

There are many types of Total Voids in the known universe. The most common is the TV. I once played with the knob on the side marked *brightness* but the programing didn't get any smarter. For lots of people the TV is the kiss of death for creativity and the fertilizer in the garden of procrastination. My advice is to be fearful of the TV. It can suck the life out of you. But, at the same time, I like TV. What a conundrum. My advice—plan your viewing. Turn on the TV just before the show you want to watch starts and (this part is hard) turn the dumb thing off the instant the show ends. Karl Marx said, "Religion ... is the opium of the people." To which I say, "TV is the marijuana." You should even beware of "educational" television. Do you really need to watch a show about the mating rituals of the fruit fly at 2:00 AM? Not if you will be tired tomorrow and frustrated that you are behind in something significantly more important to your real life than fly humping (unless you're a horny fruit fly, that is. If so watch on!).

The second Total Void is drugs, with alcohol and pot being the most common avoidance tools. Most people find that drugs and task completion don't go together. I'm told regularly something like, "I work better a little buzzed." My observations of life, along with all the brain research I have studied, disagree with that contention.

A third Total Void is small talk. Lots of people use small talk and gossip to fill their lives versus improving their lives with accomplishments. When I worked at County Mental Health earlier in my career, I was amazed how many people showed up to work at 8:00 AM to visit, drink coffee, fix their makeup, eat a donut, complain about their weight, and gossip about others who were not present. Then around 9:15 they started work. These same individuals were quick to bitch about their hefty work load at every opportunity. I have heard similar stories from numerous types of businesses across America. I would guess that there are billions of dollars in lost productivity in our nation's workplaces because of small talk and coffee.

In the area of Total Void, everyone has to decide for themselves what is more important to them—life accomplishments or avoiding life. I'm very liberal minded, it's your life ... what ya gonna do?

NEED FOR PERFECTION

Many people have a need to do everything at the highest level of accuracy. As a result they are paralyzed when it comes time to get started. If you find your self-talk saying, "There is no way I can get that looking the way it needs to look because ..." or "I can't get it that polished in only ..." you are destroying your own creative powers.

A good rule of thumb is to do the best you can in the time allotted. I find that people do amazingly well with a 90% goal versus a 100% goal. Ninety percent is still 'A' work, but not perfect. Depending on the task, even 'C' work may be good enough.

If your goal is to be a good athlete, but you are not the one in a million superstar of your sport, then maybe it is more reasonable to be a 'C' athlete who gets good exercise, enjoys companionship, and loves winning at your skill level. The alternative would be not playing tennis because you are naturally a 'C' tennis player. Check your attitude.

Max came to my office because he was having anxiety attacks. One day he had trouble breathing and went to the emergency room because he feared a heart attack. After much testing he was assured that he hadn't had a heart attack, but that if he kept up his present level of personal stress, he probably would have a heart attack in his mid forties. Max was twenty three when I met him. He was working at a full time job and spending the rest of his awake time writing a computer game program. It came down to that he lived on coffee and snack cakes, slept little and pushed himself to the max (sorry about the pun).

As it turned out, Max was close to marketing his game on three occasions in the previous 18 months. Each time he thought he was ready, he read in a computer game magazine that someone else had tweaked their product in some way so that Max felt he had to "better" that tweak in his program. At this rate Max was never going to get his product to market. His need to produce the perfect game meant that his program would never see the glow of a monitor.

Max explained, "This program is my life ... I can't put out a second rate product, it has to be the best."

So, I ask you, would it be better for Max to release a very good program, let's say an 'A-96%' program and later put out version A.1 then A.2, or for Max to keep playing with his mouse like a computerized hamster?

TIME MANAGEMENT AND PERSONAL ORGANIZATION SKILLS

Time management is really personal value management. You need to choose one task over another. Should you do your homework, or should you watch TV? Should you start to go through your stacks of boring receipts for your tax preparer, or should you go on-line and chat up some cyber sex toy?

In fact, it is much more complicated than just one choice. Literally, it is to do one task over every other task on the planet. If you choose to go and feed the homeless, you are choosing not to do everything else. If you choose to sleep in, you choose not to do every other conceivable choice that you could do. You need to manage your time through your personal values.

If a friend asks you to go fishing and you decline because you have to go to work, you are choosing work over fishing. You are placing more value on going to work than you are on going fishing. Your values need to be clear in your own mind. Only when your values are clear within your thoughts can you make choices that are correct for you.

Prior to planning your time, you have to decide what really matters to you. By knowing what you want, you force behaviors upon yourself. For example, are you willing to invest eleven years in higher education to be a nuclear physicist or a medical doctor? Are you willing to devote ten years to the piano to become a concert caliber pianist? In addition to the time, are you capable of being a nuclear physicist, medical doctor, or concert pianist?

HONEST LIMITATIONS

We have all heard it millions of times, "You can do anything you put your mind to." The reason for this type of touchy-feely statement is to encourage individuals not to give up too easily. At the dojo I workout at, one of the Black Belts likes to spout that very saying. "You can do anything you put your mind to." One day I pointed out that the saying was hollow even if he meant well. He backed his belief with all his heart.

"I tell the kids that they can make it, that they are great and that I believe in them. They just have to believe in themselves!"

"I think I can prove you wrong." I smiled.

"You just don't believe in the kids like I do!"

"I believe in you, please hold your breath for ten minutes."

Just because you want something doesn't mean that it will happen. What you have to watch out for is quitting on yourself before you have really investigated all the options.

When I was starting junior high school many of my friends were enthusiastic about becoming astronauts. The American space program was getting lots of attention and my friends were looking towards the heavens with hopeful eyes. One particular lunch period I became the butt of jokes because I announced that I had no desire to go to work at NASA. I was afraid of heights and space seemed pretty high off the ground to me. (I still don't want to be an astronaut, but I wouldn't mind a Star Trek type space shuttle to buzz around in.) I bring this up because part of knowing yourself is knowing your limitations. My fear of heights has also limited my desire to be an elevator repair man, a balloonist, or a window washer. If you are five foot one in all directions, your pro basketball career looks doomed. But your love of basketball could lead you to the broadcast booth or to write for a sports magazine. More on this later.

Your personal values set the stage for your activities. If it is your belief that life is short and to be cherished, you won't waste time well. If you believe that life is cheap and everlasting, what you do with any particular moment or afternoon doesn't matter much to you.

PREDICTING TIME

Once I was driving with my family over the bridge into the San Francisco Bay area. When I got to the toll both area there was a commotion. My family and I were driving in the free direction. Motorists in the other direction had to stop and pay a toll. From what I could tell, a car was sideways and smashed into the protective barrier in front of the toll both. Another car was smashed into the first car. Then another car, and another. It looked like eight or ten cars were trying to share the exact same space. Many cars were now stopping. As I continued onto the bridge I could see miles and miles of cars that were soon to be stuck due to the accident ahead of them. I turned back to my sons and said, "I can predict the future of those drivers."

"What?" One son questioned.

"You and I know more about their lives than they do. We know that in a minute or so they are going to be in a huge traffic jam."

At that moment, off in the distance, my son pointed out a small red flashing vehicle. A little later we passed an emergency vehicle as it went towards the accident. The emergency vehicle was moving all of twenty miles an hour along the shoulder of the road. In no time the traffic jam was miles long. When we got to San Jose, two hours later, KGO radio was still talking about the terrible traffic mess caused by the drunk driver who hit the toll booth.

This story illustrates that it is possible, in certain circumstances, to be able to predict the future. I know that, if all goes well at 7:00 o'clock this evening, I will pick up son #1 at soccer practice and at 7:15 I will pick up son #2 at the dojo. How do I know that? Because it is written on my daily schedule for today. It states:

3:00 PM   Work on Life Law #8
7:00 PM   Pick up Ethan @ Soccer
7:15 PM   Pick up Josh @ JuJitsu.

If all goes well, at 6:45 I will be closing down the computer and heading for the car. Soccer is 10 minutes away from my office. At 7:00 I should be picking up a sweaty, red faced teenager... and so on.

I know all this because I keep a day planner. Nothing fancy, but it is very important for my life's organization. I have kept one since high school. I have a few simple rules for planning my days, and as long as I don't break my own rules I tend to get lots done with a minimum of personal grief.

"Stop, wait a minute!" You might be saying, "A daily planner? Isn't that for busy executives? I'm not a rich business man with lots to do. I'm not a dork with a fancy day planner."

You may not be a rich executive, but you are busy. You do have a life. You do have things to plan.

Don't let the day planner throw you. What I want to discuss with you is a tool to help you get your needs met. It is personal. It is about you and your needs.

If you knew that at seven tonight you were going to be in a huge traffic jam, on a bridge, in earthquake country, would you try to avoid the situation? Well, in a personal way, my daily calendar focuses me on what I want to accomplish and how important, to me, each task is. I try to use my 86,400 seconds to the fullest. I work hard and I play hard. What I don't do is worry hard. I have noticed however, that people do a lot of worrying about forgetting things.

I think of planning in the same way cows eat. When a cow chows down on some sweet clover, she chomps away and fills up one of her four stomachs. Then, later on, she goes and hangs out over there and chews her cud. What she is doing is bringing up lunch and re-chewing the really fibrous stuff again, and maybe again. This sounds nasty (and it is), but for the cow it is the best way to get all the nutrition out of her fibrous diet. In cow speak, this is called rumination, the act of chewing cud.

Lots of people also ruminate. They bring up stuff all day and make sure that they keep it their mind. Some people worry all day and all night long. So, if you have a meeting at say 4:00, you keep it on your mind throughout your entire day. You think of it at 1:15. You ruminate at 2:37 and again at 3:11. Now that takes a lot of brain power. In fact, I contend it takes a lot of <u>wasted</u> brain power.

Virgil was very upset. He was angry with himself for forgetting an appointment.

Virgil: Yesterday I was supposed to go and put in an application for a new job. I talked to the manager last week and he said he would be happy to talk to me. I politely asked him to commit to a time. I was all excited about the interview. I just simply forgot.

Dr. Phil: You forgot?

Virgil: Yeah. I was thinking about it all week. I was looking forward to the interview. At about six last night it dawned on me that I forgot.

Dr. Phil: You didn't forget. You remembered at six. You remembered at the wrong time.

Virgil: I hadn't thought about it like that. I guess I didn't really forget.

Virgil was blaming his memory. But in fact, it was not his memory that was faulty. It was the tool he used to trigger his memory.

Virgil: At around three I went off with friends to hang. I wasn't doing anything.

Dr. Phil: You were doing something. You were hanging out with your friends.

What Virgil needed was a plan. He thought he had one, but it proved not to work very well for him. So now he needs a better plan. He needs to have some way for him to trigger his own memory so that he can do a particular behavior, like go to the job interview, at a particular time.

Repetitive worry is a poor tool for keeping organized. We tend to be able to ruminate only when we are not involved with some meaningful act, like during math class, or a boring meal, or when we should be sleeping. When we are with friends, all involved with the entertainment value of the interaction, time goes by. The more involved we are the quicker time goes by. Thus, at six o'clock Virgil brought back up his cud and started chewing. Then he remembered, *4:00 Interview.* You snooze you lose, the saying goes. Unfortunately, when Virgil called to try to set up another interview, the manager didn't return his calls.

EXCUSES/LIES

Over the years I have noticed that most people react to their life, versus controlling their life. If you do not plan your days you will be dealing with stuff as it occurs, you will need to be reactive. If you plan your day you have large portions of time during which you are in control. Not every minute, but lots of minutes. You will be proactive. You will be choosing your path. This is important to me. I hate to be told what to do. I like to tell myself what to do. Whenever possible I want to be proactive. If I had been stuck on the other side of the highway in the earlier story, I would have had little choice but to be stuck in a traffic jam. I couldn't wish the auto accident away. But, I could have had proactive choices about how I reacted to the sudden change in my plans, a change that I had little to do with. I might have chosen to visit with my family, but after hours in the car, well, we would probably be all visited out. I might have tried to find an impromptu card game or read or check through mail or write a letter. I know that I cannot always control my life, so I actually plan for inconvenience. When we travel I bring reading materials, cards, a chess game, paper and pens. I take reading material that is important to me when I go to the doctor's office so I am not stuck reading whatever I can find. I have often joked to friends, "As soon as I am stuck somewhere, I'm going to ..." What I am really saying is, that at this moment I am too busy to do whatever it is right now, but I would like to. So, when some unscheduled time drops in my lap, I'm going to. Over the years I have noticed that people have lots of excuses for not planning their day. I politely call them excuses, but really I think of them as personal lies. Let's look at some of the biggies.

I'M TOO BUSY TO PLAN

This is the most common excuse. "Who has time to do that every day?" The answer: People who wish to get stuff done! If you won $86,400 dollars would you spend fifteen minutes planning what you were going to do with it? I surely would, in fact a lot longer. And, I would enjoy playing with the thoughts of what I could do

Dost thou love life? Then do not squander time, for that's the stuff life is made of.

Benjamin Franklin

with the money.

Well, you have 86,400 seconds tomorrow, what are you going to do with them? At this point you might be thinking, a second is very small. Who cares! You're right, but what second are you thinking about? If you hold your breath for ten seconds, no big whoop. But, after two minutes every second is really noticeable. I suspect that each second you hold your breath you will get more respect for the "insignificant" second. If you have no plan for yourself tomorrow, you are giving yourself permission to be reactive every second of the day.

A daily plan puts you in control of your time. A valuable commodity that you cannot replace.

I HATE NOT BEING FREE, A DAILY PLANNER IS CONTROLLING

A daily planner is controlling, self controlling. You are indeed responsible for controlling yourself (see Chapters 1-3).

My daily planner is my behavioral map to success. As I have told you before, I am basically lazy. If I didn't control my basic desire to butt hug my couch and watch TV, I would be the best couch potato on planet Earth. In my daily planner I plan work, play and *do nothing* time. When I am following my plan I am not feeling guilty because I know that I planned my day according to my values. I plan based on what I believe is correct for me. I plan towards my own personal definition of success. I guarantee I will not pass judgement on how you define your personal success as long as you are not hurting other people and you are feeling creative. It is your life, create with it.

MY LIFE IS BORING, I HAVE NOTHING TO PLAN

Everyone has a routine life. Often this can feel boring. But it is not routine or boring—it is life. If you're bored, you are boring. Why would you want to be boring? Spice up your life.

George hated his Monday through Friday mornings. He was a high school senior and ready to go to college, but he still had months to go before he was a high school graduate. His grades were good and he was already accepted for college. He was tread-

We must use time as a tool, not as a couch.

John F. Kennedy

> *My daily planner is my behavioral map to success.*
> Philip Copitch, Ph.D.

ing water. A week after we talked he told me that he had found a book of seldom used words. He had been carrying it with him in has backpack. When he found that he had a few wasted minutes he would flip open the book and try to learn one new word. He started asking his friends what they thought the word meant and it had led to a game. One teacher even asked him where he got the book (garage sale, 25¢). George was playing mind candy. Something small and sweet to make something out of nothing. Earth shattering? No. But a valuable use of time for a man who wants to be a sports writer.

PLANNING DOESN'T WORK FOR ME, I ALREADY TRIED IT ONCE

My Uncle Joe once told me, *If you fish in the desert you won't snag your line, but you won't find fish either.* Uncle Joe was a strange old bird, but what I think he was teaching me is that a bad plan is just as bad as no plan.

It takes a little bit of practice to find a system that works for you. There are lots of planners sold in office supply stores that seem to be an OK starting place. But, what I found was that they did not work for me. They were designed to work well for everybody, but I am just a single body. So over the years I begged, borrowed, and stole the best of lots of planners and simplified all of these into one that works well for me. I do mean simplified. Most of the "systems" I have seen are a six week course within themselves to get me to fit into their planner. That is not my style. I like my world more simple, less flash (remember, I am basically lazy).

Over the next few pages I will explain one simple way that lots of people have found useful. I advise that you try it for a day or two, then play with it and make it yours. It isn't fancy, but it is functional. This little plan has made me lots of money too. I have used it for years to organize my world.

> *To choose time is to save time.*
> Francis Bacon

As I said earlier, my daily planner is my behavioral map to success. Success in the broadest sense of the word.

DR. PHIL'S TWO SHEET SIMPLE PLANNER

My planner consists of two pages of 8 1/2 by 11 inch copy paper. Page one has the hours of the day and check boxes followed by a short line for small tasks. I have one full week at a time on that page (some people like planners that are laid out one page per day which gives them lots of little chunks of time). Page two is full of lots of lines and wide open space to jot notes and thoughts down. That's it. I guess it uses about 5¢ worth of paper. I made mine up on a computer and copy it over and over onto 3 hole punched paper. I keep it stored in a three ring binder. Originally it was a plastic one, but now I have a cool leather binder I received as a birthday present (20 birthdays ago). I write the dates in by hand and double check that I am doing it correctly. I keep three months of calendar paper in my binder at a time. I choose not to plan out past about a month. Far away plans like weddings or vacations I keep on a monthly calendar in the back of the binder. Pretty simple. Let's look at each part and how it works.

Section A and Section B

43,252,003,274,489,856,00 is the number of different color combinations on a Rubik's Cube (in short hand math speak, that's only 43+ quintillion, and still less complicated than dealing with your mother).

SECTION A: HOURS OF THE DAY - THE CHUNKS

When I commit to doing something that is time related I write it down, in pencil, on the correct line (I do mean "correct" line. If you are not careful, you will show up at the wrong time. Embarrassing, done it!). I write it in pencil because things change. If need be I can move things around.

If you and I commit to getting together at say, 3:00 PM Thursday, May 27, I would go to that day in my planner and write it in. I print so that I can read it on May 27th. I may also jot a short note to myself to jog my memory.

3:00 PM Loyal Reader / talk about planner

This does two important things for me. It lets me forget about Loyal Reader until May 27th and it will jog my memory about our last conversation. This is important. If I have to keep track of everything in my mind, I will end up completely stressed out. Also, I will never really be able to focus on what I am doing in the present. As we will discuss later, this lack of focus dooms most people to being mediocre.

I have a huge Must Rule, **I do not commit to anything without my planner.** I keep my planner close by—but safe. If I'm in the dojo getting my ass kicked, my planner is in my car. If I'm at work, my planner is at work. If I'm at home, my planner is at home. My planner is an extension of my frontal lobe. It is part of my brain matter. If I lose my planner, I am fishing in the desert; I'm royally screwed.

Parkinson's Law

Work expands to fill the time available for its completion

C. Northcote Parkinson

I also write projects in my planner. Such as:

JuJitsu
Lunch with Geri
Pick up Josh
Write report / Smith, A

I schedule my life. I write specifically what I will be doing and when. If I just said to myself, "I need to get some exercise later today", I would just keep putting it off all day (I'm still basically lazy!). I would justify my way out of doing it. But, when I have a planned meeting with myself, I do it. So I set a specific plan and write it in my planner, "3:00 JuJitsu." Then I go do it. It is in my plan, the one I set for myself based on my personal values. I am in control of my life whenever possible.

If I put on my "Do List": *Write report / Smith, A.* I now have to find a time slot when I should do it. If it is only in my mind's worry list it is very easy to keep putting it off (the "Do List," Section B, will be discussed on the next page).

I plan things that count: meetings, quiet time, drive time, naps. If I think I should do it, I plan it. I also plan obligations, responsibilities and wishes. Every month I plan, *Write Checks,* a task I detest, but I don't want to forget to pay the electric bill. In my business I pay my bills around the 25th day of the month. I will know which day, because every night I review my upcoming days. I plan which day I will tackle the bills, either the 23rd, 24th, 25th, or 26th, depending on other obligations in the flow of the business month. On a few occasions I have, unfortunately, had to do it at midnight on the 26th. Not my first choice, but for that particular month it was my best choice.

You may have noticed that my day starts at 10:00 AM and ends at 10:00 PM. Remember this is <u>my</u> planner. It is customized for me. I find that I'm stupid before 10:00 AM so I avoid pre-ten as much as possible. Your calendar should reflect your life. I have a friend who loves 5:00 AM. He tells me, "It's quiet, I get my best work done when I'm fresh." I have no idea how he does it. There is only one five on my clock.

You make your daily planner fit your life-style and make sure you can get your sleep.

SECTION B: SMALL ITEM CHECK BOXES.

On page one, next to the hours of the day, I keep my Small Item Check Box List. Most people call it a "To Do List." I tend to think of it as a "DO List." I like to be proactive, I get things done (self-talk slipping out a bit there).

I put things on the Small Item Check Box List page that tend to take less than ten minutes or bigger things needing to be assigned a time slot.

For example, I may have three phone calls that I would like to make. Each might take five minutes. If I did them all at once, I would need at least fifteen minutes to get all three done. Or, as it may turn out, the people aren't by their phones so I get nothing done in fifteen minutes.

What I do is keep my small stuff handy. When a chunk of time opens up, I grab one of these little projects and I get it done. So, if my five

Nothing is ours except time.

Seneca

o'clock appointment is late by ten minutes, I'll use the 600 seconds given back to me. I leverage my time. This leveraged time adds up to hundreds of hours every year (it feels like found time, but we know that we only get 86,400 seconds per day).

Instead of staring out of the window, or feeling rejected by the late arrival, I use the time to complete a small task. Throughout my week I will leverage time to:

Open junk mail (I like it)
Make a quick call
Read short articles
Read part of a longer article
Write a thank you note (I have a lot to be thankful for so I write lots
    of thank you notes.)
Pick up messages
Stretch my lower back (I'm getting old)
And, my favorite, pee!

This type of "small stuff" takes up a lot of time. So, I use my time wisely. If I'm waiting my turn at the doctor's office, I have a book to read. If I'm stuck—I get little things done. I plan for it, life is inconvenient, so I can find lots of leverage seconds floating throughout my week.

Section C

SECTION C: THE BIG STUFF

The page I call the Big Stuff is for big stuff that I want to do but I can't or don't want to assign a specific time to doing it. If I get

The now the here, through which all future plunges into the past.

James Joyce
Ulysses

an idea, hear an interesting saying, or think of a *wish I could,* I jot it down on this page. Most of the stories and sayings in this book started life on the Big Stuff page. Stuff stays on this page until I find a better home for it.

For example: the cartoon at the beginning of Chapter 4 started out as a punch line that I hastily wrote down during a meeting. The presenter was very boring and my mind wandered. It tripped over the punch line somewhere during its wanderings and I wrote it down.

A few days later, as I was planning my day, I went down the battered page of Big Stuff and made sure that I had found homes for all the stuff that had ended up on it. The last thing I did was to cut out the punch line. Then, I threw the rest of the page away, and dropped the punch line into a red plastic box in my den. The red plastic box is the repository for all potential cartoons. There it sat for months.

One day, months later, I was on the phone with an insurance company. I was trying to get them to pay for therapy for a kid who needed it. I got placed on hold. While listening to the 'on hold music' I checked out my red fun basket. As I read over the first few notes I wondered how I ever thought that they were funny. I tossed them into the trash. Then I found the punch line *"Even if I get Alzheimer's, I'll remember what you just said!"* and played with it in my head. Out of leveraged "phone hell" time I found a usable cartoon. Sure beats just listening to the phone-hold band.

The Big Stuff page tends to be the repository of stuff I have hope in. My page today has these three time consuming listings:

Birthday present for Geri
Find garage floor
Drop dead trees

These are not tasks—these are part time jobs. But I still need/ want to do them. In three weeks my bride is going to have another birthday. After an eternity together, what do you get the woman who has everything and always says, "I don't need anything but time with my family." Or, "Whenever I suggest what I want for my birthday you always say, 'That's not a real present, just go get that yourself!'" Finding a cool present is going to

When Thomas Edison was asked the secret of his success he replied:

"I work incessantly on one task for a long time without weary."

When asked to explain he said:

"Most people do lots of things in their sixteen hour day. I take the time in question and apply it in one direction to one object."

be difficult.

The garage is a nuclear waste site without the radiation. Organizing it is at least an eight hour job. I haven't had eight free hours to "waste" on a garage in ???? Actually, never have, but I would like it cleaned up.

I have twenty dead or dying trees just off the driveway. Pine Beetle I am told. This is probably a forty hour job that needs to be done. I need to dry out the trees by sawing them up to interrupt the two year life cycle of the little beasties.

My job will be to break these tasks down into manageable parts and take on each part. Please notice none of these big jobs are "work" related. These are life related tasks. I don't just plan my work day (or school day), I plan my life. That way I get stuff done.

Another thing on my Big Stuff list was *Call Barbara about time of Red Cross meeting.* This ended up there when Barbara called and left a message asking about the meeting. I put the note next to a check box and forgot about it. I was really busy when I got the message, so I put the message in a safe place.

At the end of my day I will take ten minutes to plan for tomorrow. I will check down the lists and move stuff that needs to be moved. Tonight Barbara will go from the big stuff and notes list to the small stuff today list. Tomorrow during leveraged time I will call Barbara and tell her the time of the meeting. (Interesting note: Barbara and I were both in the room when the Red Cross meeting was scheduled. I wrote it down and forgot it. Barbara planned on remembering it, but now isn't sure and called me. Sweet lady, but disorganized.)

WHAT ELSE IS IN THE PLANNER BINDER

· I keep a pencil
· My phone book (Print out from my computer. Updated whenever I remember to do it. Usually twice a year.)
· Plain paper
· Up to twenty pieces of paper to read. An article cut out of a magazine, a letter with a map I will need next week, and jokes or articles people give me. This is for leveraging time if I'm stuck away from my normal haunts (Waiting for kids after school, waiting for a meeting to start). I've leveraged time at all sorts of places. Movie theaters, baseball games, waiting for a friend in the hospital to wake up and visit with me. One kid called me an intellectual Boy Scout. I guess I am.

All my possessions for a moment of time.

Elizabeth I
Last words

WHAT TO AVOID

I suggest you avoid sticky notes, scraps of paper, the backs of envelopes, or writing on yourself. All these types of notes tend to get lost or washed or build on themselves. Sticky pads were a great money maker for 3M but do not really help people stay organized.

TEN MINUTE PLANNING TIME EVERY DAY

If you use the simple two page planner described above, you will find that you get lots more done. Mainly because you are clearly aware of what you wish to accomplish today, so you have a chance to get it done.

Probably the best thing the simple two page planner does for people is it relieves worry. Worry? Yes worry. Many people spend lots of time worrying about forgetting stuff or getting stuff done. Lots of people have a hard time going to sleep at night because they play their next day over and over in their minds, hoping not to screw something up. This is emotionally draining and dysfunctional.

> *You got to be intense when it counts.*
> Arthur Ashe

For example: If I want to call Bob tomorrow, I write it on my Small Item do list and don't think about it until my next planning time. My planning time is the last ten minutes of my "work" day. At the end of my day, whenever that is, I open my planner and look over tomorrow. I read down Section A and make sure that I understand what I expect out of myself. I double check things like drive time or location. If I have a 3:00 at my office, I make sure that I can be at my office before 3:00. If I have to be across town, I make sure I have the "drive time" calculated correctly so I can be on time. I double check that I have what I need for my set appointments.

Next, I look down my Section B. I appoint larger items to open time slots. So, if I have a report to read for my 3:00 meeting, I appoint 30 minutes to read the report at 11:00. I move the item from my Do List to a time slot. It is now an appointment. I have an appointment with a stack of paper. With experience I have learned about how long it takes me to read a page, so I allot my time accordingly. If tomorrow at 10:50 a friend calls and invites me to coffee, I will check my calendar and politely decline, "I have an appointment at 11:00. I can't get away right now." At 3:00 when I attend my meeting I will be a lot happier with myself because I read the report, rather than had a cup of coffee with a friend. At 10:50 I may have wanted to go for coffee, but I attended the appointment that I made with myself to prepare for my 3:00.

I never explain why I can't sneak off for coffee. I simply state the fact, "I have an appointment." No guilt involved. I am not disrespecting my friend, I am staying focused. I have an appointment. When I hear people explain themselves it makes me think of them as weak minded.

"I'd love to go for coffee with you, but I can't. I have to read a report for my 3:00 today. I'm sorry."

I've even heard people try to talk their friends out of doing what they should do.

"AAAH, come on! You can glance over the report later on. It'll only take a few minutes. I really want to have coffee with you!"

This seems selfish to me. His want for coffee is more important than your want to accomplish your task. True friends don't sabotage your goals, they advocate and support them.

Some people like to start their day with a planning session. They start off fresh and they organize their day. I advocate that you plan at the end of your day. That way you don't need to worry about tomorrow because it is all planned. However, if you are really a morning person, it makes sense to do your planning then. The most important part of the ten minute planning session is that you truly focus on what you want to get done. For those ten minutes you are 100% focused on the task of prioritizing your day.

APPOINTING BIG PROJECTS

Big projects often cover days or even months. Lots, if not most people, find big projects overwhelming. For some this feeling is so powerful that it immobilizes them and keeps them from achieving their life goals.

In the real world, big or bigger projects have to be dealt with. They cannot be avoided. They need special care. I advise you to deal with big projects *backwards*.

Let's use an example of a term paper (It could be any big project like planning a wedding, organizing a school fund-raiser, or developing your career). This term paper is a big deal, 50% of your grade. Today is April 9th and it is due April 30th. You have known about the paper all semester, but finally, today, the instructor defined the parameters of the damn thing. So you turn to April 30/2:00 PM and write: Hand in Term Paper, Psychology 310.

For most people this makes their chest tight. Lots of thoughts cross their minds. Some think, "I've got lots of time, I'll worry about it next week." Others think, "I only have a few weeks, I'll never get this done, why did I sign up for this damn class!" But, a big but here—an organized mind thinks, "Another task. Lots of parts. How am I going to break this task down so I can kick ass on this term paper?"

A big project can feel like an elephant was shoved down your throat. A big project can feel like it is going to choke you.

So, *how do you eat an elephant?*

One bite at a time. If when you put that piece into your mouth it is still too big, and it's choking you, you spit it out and cut it up some more. The trick (or art) to dealing with big projects is to make them into lots of small projects. Once they are small ones, you organize dealing with them backwards. Read on, it will become clearer in a few minutes.

I wasted time, and now doth time waste me.

William Shakespeare
Richard II

Your assignment is to write a term paper on how children learn. It kind of sounds interesting, but you don't know squat about how kids learn. Your first thought is "...they go to school." But, unfortunately, that isn't much of a term paper. I'm going to take you through the process. We are not going to actually set up the term paper, we are only going to look at the process. (This book isn't the place for a How To on term papers. If you need information on how to write one however, go to my web site, www.CopitchInc.com, and look under Recommended Links. You will find lots of helpful information for high school and college students stuck with study problems.)

What you will need is your Datebook, a pencil, and a monthly calendar with squares for every day.

The facts—

Today's date is: April 9th

The report is due: April 30th

You have 22 days to learn about and write a great report (1,900,800 seconds).

Before this report was assigned, you had a pretty full life already. It is going to take some organization skills to use your time to its fullest and get this report done on time.

What do you have to do to write a great report, and how long will each part take? When it comes to the project time be realistic, not hopeful. If you schedule too much time, great—you're done with time left to do something else. But, if you schedule too little time, you're screwed! You can't make more so you're all stressed out trying to figure out who or what you are going to screw time out of.

Parts of the Big Project:	Estimated Time
Research the subject	(8.00 hours)
Organize research into outline	(3.00 hours)
Expand on outline into paragraph form	(4.00 hours)
Type first draft of report	(4.00 hours)
Give draft to proofreader	(0.25 hours)
Pick up draft from proofreader	(0.25 hours)
Make changes to draft	(1.00 hours)
Research to fill gaps in paper (polish)	(2.00 hours)
Type changes and further polish	(2.00 hours)
Give second draft to proofreader	(0.25 hours)
Pick up second draft from proofreader	(0.25 hours)
Make final changes, put project to bed	(1.00 hours)
Print out final paper	(0.50 hours)
Total:	26.50 hours

It will take you 26.50 hours to do a great job on this report. The next question is when?

The Future is something which everyone reaches at the rate of sixty minutes an hour, whatever he does, whoever he is.
C.S. Lewis
The Screwtape Letters

April 2002

Sunday	Monday	Tuesday	Wednesday	Thursday	Friday	Saturday
	1	2	3	4	5	6
7	8	9	10	11	12	13
14	15	16	17	18	19	20
21	22	23	24	25	26	27
28	29	30				

Organizing big projects backwards in small chunks on a monthly calendar

I recommend that we organize your big project time backwards. We start with April 30th. In the square for April 30th write, Hand in Term Paper, Psychology 310, 2:00 PM. Your monthly calendar now is in sync with your daily planner (*Hand in Term Paper, Psychology 310*, is written in the 2:00 time slot).

Before we go any further, what big events are scheduled in your life from April 9th to April 30th? On the 28th you are planning to go to Sally and Tom's wedding. That day is shot for studying, but the wedding should be fun. Write *Sally and Tom's Wedding* in the April 28th square. In fact, while you're at it, you need to write, *Buy present for Sally and Tom*, on your daily planner. You can't go to the wedding empty handed.

Back to April 30th. What would be the very last thing you would need to do before you could *Hand in Term Paper, Psychology 310, 2:00 PM?* Think small chunks.

You need to print the completed paper out of the computer. When would you like to do that? Don't say April 29th at 11:59 PM. That is cutting it too close. That is stress inducing. That could put you in a terrible spot. What if at 11:59 PM on April 29th your printer dies, or the electricity goes out, or you have the trudging trots from the cheap food at Sally and Tom's wedding? Shit happens. Murphy's Law says: *What can go wrong, will go wrong and usually at the worst possible time.* The worst possible time for this term paper would be 11:59 PM on April 29th. You don't need that aggravation. Planning is supposed to make your life less stressful. Wouldn't it be a lot less stressful if on Saturday, April 27th, you printed out the paper? Assuming all goes well, you're three days ahead of schedule. I guarantee that is stress lowering. Also, when you're at the wedding, you can relax and have a great time. If the paper isn't done, you may find yourself stressing over it and not focusing on fun.

On Saturday, April 27th, write: *Print out finished paper.* In parentheses put in the time it will take you to get this done: 30 minutes.

Now you take all the parts from above and place them into your monthly calendar. Keep in mind your nature and your other commitments. For example, if you work long hours on Wednesdays, it would be unrealistic to come home and throw yourself into a valuable term paper. Also, be realistic on how much you can really do on one project at a time. Most people can really focus for about four hours. So, if you plan on doing eight or twelve hours of work one day, you'll probably only get four powerful hours out of your brain.

In the appropriate squares write the following:

April 27: Pick up second draft from proofreader (0.25 hours)

Make final changes, put project to bed (1.00 hours)

Print out final paper (0.50 hours)

April 26: Give second draft to proofreader (0.25 hours)

April 25: Research to fill gaps in paper (polish) (2.00 hours)

Type changes and further polish (2.00 hours)

April 23: Pick up draft from proofreader (0.25 hours)

Make changes to draft (1.00 hours)

April 21:   Give draft to proofreader (0.25 hours)

April 20:   Type first draft of report (4.00 hours)

April 18:   Expand on outline into paragraph form (4.00 hours)

April 14:   Organize research into outline (3.00 hours)

April 13:   Research the subject (4.00 hours)

April 11:   Research the subject (4.00 hours)

Once this is done and it looks realistic for you and your skills, appoint it into your daily planner. Now you're acting organized.

LET'S LOOK AT A FEW STICKY PLACES IN THE BIG PROJECT ORGANIZATION:

Make sure you understand that rewrite is a major part of writing. Do not plan on your report flowing easily from your mind to paper. Writing is work. A common statement between writers is, "I sat at my computer and slit my wrists!" You will have to rewrite, and for most people the rewrite is as hard and time consuming as the first writing.

You will need to have a competent proofreader or two. You wrote what is on the paper, so when you try to proof your own work, you know what is supposed to be written. Often you will read what you meant to write, missing the little mistakes. If you have to be your own proofreader, put your paper down for at least a day. This will give your mind a chance to really read what you have on the page. If you read your own work out loud slowly, you have a better chance of catching errors.

Before you give your work to the proofreader, make sure it is ready. Your proofreader is not supposed to fix your shoddy paper, she is supposed to be "a set of new eyes" to catch mistakes.

You need to respect your proofreader. You cannot expect your proofreader to drop everything to proof your work. It is usually best to set an appointment to have your work proofed. If your proofreader states that she can do it, "Wednesday night", it is your job to have it to her before she is ready for it. This takes some planning and coordination. Often college students trade off proofing each others papers. You need to appoint when she will have the proofed paper returned. Your project will come to a halt if the proofreader can't get to your paper. It is crucial to have a good working relationship with your proofreader.

One last thing about working with your proofreader. Don't take their advice personally. If your paper comes back with lots of red marks, it is not a character attack on you. It is the normal process of rewrite. It is much better to fix the mistakes than to turn them in and get a lower grade. A good proofreader is hard to find, so when you find one, treat her like a trusted advisor.

SOMETIMES LIFE GETS IN THE WAY.

What if you are down with the flu on April 25th? You have no choice but to rework your schedule. It is usually pretty easy to rework your schedule if you have planned it well from the get go. The rule of thumb is to try not to move stuff around too much to fix a problem. In your present schedule you have 1.5 hours of work to do on April 25th. You need to find that time somewhere before April 26th at 6:00 PM when you are scheduled to give the paper to the proofreader. If you have to bump the proofreader's time back, you are looking for trouble. What if the proofreader can't get to your paper in a timely fashion?

Sometimes you have a block of time open up. Let's say Friday, April 19th your date falls through. You now have all evening to fill. You find that you're kind of in a funk. It would be easy to watch TV all night and snack on junk food. But, what if you used this free time to get ahead? You could start on the April 20th work. It will get your mind off your lacking love life and fill you with feelings of accomplishment. OK, it may not be all that, but you won't have anything to show for watching TV all evening (except a few more ounces on your butt), so taking control may actually feel good. It is a way of getting more time. Your cancelled date is found time. Also, if you are done with April 20th's work, you can plan something else (no, not TV) or start working on April 21st's part of the project. You should not give yourself permission to not do your assigned work, but it feels good to be ahead of the project. And, if you get the flu, you won't be too screwed up (Murphy's Law demands the flu on real busy and project vital days).

JUDGING TIME TAKES PRACTICE

It takes time to know how long stuff will take to do. You have to be open to learning as you go. You start off using *guesstimation* to put a project together. Then, with experience you will learn more about yourself. Some people find that two hours is the most brain power they can give at one sitting. So this person will need to schedule two sessions at the library, maybe on the same day, with a lunch in between or a class. Know thyself and don't work against your own abilities.

SUPERFLUITY

REID:

I am extremely adept at squandering time, probably more so than most people. Recently, I sat down and tried to remember what exactly I had accomplished or taken care of the previous afternoon, or the one before that, and I really couldn't recall what I had done. It's not that I have a lack of things that need to be taken care of. For countless afternoons, I have gotten home from school or work at 2:00 or 3:00 and unconsciously decided that my day was more or less over.

There are a lot of distractions around me; the phone rings, I pick up a motorcycle magazine, I watch some Monty Python DVD's and there goes several hours of potentially productive time where I could have been getting things done. Instead I switched my brain off. It has really been a struggle for me to shift my own clock, realize that my obligations don't end once I'm home, and that I still have a couple of hours after dinner to unwind.

9. Life's Law #9

Invest in yourself

"That is not exactly what I meant when I suggested that you should 'invest in yourself!'"

9. LIFE'S LAW #9

Invest in yourself

Life law #9 is relatively short and sweet. It consists of doing what is best for yourself and letting go of emotional prisons. In my practice I find that individuals tend to have a hard time dealing with this life law. Lots of people seem to hold on with all their emotional might to the very things that they should let go of so they can find happiness.

There are two major ways to invest in yourself: one is to add to your own skill level, and the second is to divest yourself of emotional baggage.

ADD TO YOUR OWN SKILL LEVEL

This is a straight forward statement. When you are making choices keep in mind that you are a work in progress. You need to challenge yourself towards higher skill levels. Part of making a life decision should be asking yourself the following questions:

What will I learn?
How will this help me develop stronger skills?
How can I use my new knowledge?
Who will I be around?
Will these people be a positive or negative influence on me?

Irving, age 17, visited my office because his grades had fallen from 'B's' to 'D's.' His mother was concerned that he didn't care about school any longer. Irving told me that his life was going OK and that he was bored in school because he didn't see any reason to learn all the subjects. He had a plan. He was going to work for a video game company when he graduated. He wanted to "play games all day long."

Dr. Phil: So, what are you doing to make you look good to a gaming company? I would think there are lots of applications for video development jobs.

Irving: I know all the games. I'm good at them, everyone calls me for cheats. I'm awesome on them all.

Dr. Phil: That's great, but that makes you a consumer, someone who buys computer games, not a programmer and/or author.

Irving:	I read a lot. I like to read.
Dr. Phil:	What kind of stuff?
Irving:	I read all the gaming magazines and I read lots of sci-fi books. I've seen every sci-fi movie ever made. I'm into the old black and white ones, better writing, but lame special effects.
Dr. Phil:	Let me ask you a tough question, what can you put on your job application when you go to get work at a gaming company?

This question hit Irving like a ton of bricks. He had never thought about what his life would look like on a job application or what he would look like through the eyes of an employer.

Irving is not alone. I meet lots of young adults with lots of hope but no plan. About once a month I am told by someone:

"I don't need school, I'm going to play pro ball."

"I don't need school, my old man is rich."

"I don't need school, I have big plans, I'm going to make it large in the music business."

"I don't need school, my dad never graduated and he is doing OK for himself."

To these types of statements I reply, "I can't predict the future, but it seems to me that education doesn't get in the way. It seems to me, the more you know the safer you are. I'm not necessarily talking school, but I am talking education."

In a nutshell, life goes by. Invest in yourself every day. Add to your skills. Add to your abilities. If you don't choose to invest in you, who will?

DIVEST YOURSELF OF EMOTIONAL BAGGAGE

Ali entered therapy because she was getting nothing done with her life. She was thirty and spent most of her time alone. She went to work, then went to an aerobics class, then she went home. She reported that she had no social life.

When I asked her why she had no social life she replied in a matter of fact way: "I was raped by a friend in college."

She explained:

I used to be more outgoing. I went on lots of dates. When I left home and went off to school I was very active in stuff at school. I was always invited to all the parties. I got good grades and had lots of friends. At the end of the year party my sophomore year, I got real drunk. I got so drunk I really acted out. I passed out and I was raped. End of story, I was stupid. I don't even know for sure who did it. A few days later, one of the other girls told me that she knew of three guys who were bragging about the great time they had with me. I never thought that it was more than one. I sat in my dorm room and cried for the rest of the day. I went to the school counseling center and they gave me tests, but the police said that they couldn't do anything because I didn't know who raped me.

I spent the summer at home hiding. I got angrier every day. I never told my mother. She wouldn't have understood. I told her I was unhappy and I changed schools. I thought it would be all right. I would start over.

Now I just go to work and go home. I started to gain weight, so I started doing aerobics.

After a long pause:

My life was stolen from me. I wish I could find the bastards who raped me and tell them what they did was wrong ... show them that they ruined my life, that they deserve to burn in hell. I hope they will.

Eight years later, Ali was still living the horror of her rape. She had built a prison of fear, anger, hatred, and sorrow, and locked herself within it.

Anyone can become angry—that is easy. But to be angry with the right person, to the right degree, at the right time, for the right purpose, and in the right way—this is not easy.

Aristotle

EMOTIONAL PAIN LASTS MUCH LONGER THAN THE INITIAL EVENT

A large portion of the human brain has been developed to store memories. We have the ability to recall positive and negative events. Most people find that they can remember negative events better. In fact, there is lots of evidence that it was important to our very survival that we remembered negative events. The quicker a species learns from negative events, the more likely that they will survive to produce offspring. It was, and still is today, important that we learn quickly from dangerous situations. If our ancestors had not learned about the dangers, they would have been easy dinners for predatory animals.

Our minds recall negative memories with great skill. Most of the time this is probably a good thing, but sometimes we spend so much time remembering the negative, we forget to have a life. We live with one foot stuck in the past.

EMOTIONAL PAIN INFLUENCES YOUR HEALTH

Research has shown that the process of thought influences the body at the system and cellular level. It is well documented that your thoughts influence your immune system, which in turn influences the way your body fights off disease.

Researchers at Ohio State University studied caregivers of Alzheimer's patients. The female volunteers agreed to have a large hole punched into the skin of their forearms. Another group of similarly aged woman, who did not take care of relatives with Alzheimer's had the same procedure done. It is fair to say that taking care of a relative with Alzheimer's is abnormally stressful. The caregivers (abnormal stress) healed in 49 days whereas the control group (normal stress) women healed in 39 days. It took ten more days for the women who were taking care of their ill family

The researchers at the University of New York at Stony Brook also looked at positive thoughts and overall health. They found that office workers who were criticized by their employers had a drop in illness-fighting cells for approximately one day. On the positive side, those same workers had an increase of illness fighting cells for two days if they went to a party with friends.

member to heal.

In another study researchers talked dental students into having a gash put into the roof of their mouths, twice. The first cut was placed days before the dental students took their final exams, the hardest and probably most stressful exams of their lives. The second cuts were placed weeks later, after school was out. The researchers found that it took 40% longer, on average, for the pre-test cuts to heal.

Another study found that when researchers deliberately squirted a cold virus into the nasal passages of volunteers, the volunteers who reported high stress levels developed the most colds. The volunteers with the lowest life stress stayed cold free. The researchers noted that test subjects that had an "avoidant-coping" style of dealing with stress stayed healthy. Positive self-talk is an avoidant-coping skill which distracts one from the negatives in life and helps one to focus on the positives in life.

On a side note, how do researchers talk people into allowing them to cut them or stick cold viruses up their nose? I'm glad that people volunteer for scientific studies, but pity the scientist who has to ask, "Can I stick a cold up your nose, please!"

Fortunately, the immune system is less intrusive to test. Researchers at the University of New York at Stony Brook found it took only a few minutes for illness-fighting cells to decrease when college students were placed in a stressful situation. Other researchers have found that illness fighting cells are lower in people who are taking care of ill relatives, people who worry about living next to nuclear power plants, and medical students during exam week.

It seems reasonable to assume that if you are lingering in emotional turmoil you are not supporting your own overall good health. I bring this up specifically because, if you are unable to forgive, you are allowing yourself to continue the abuse ... daily. That is an awful lot of power you are giving to the aggressor from your past. Power that you are taking from yourself. Life energy that you are wasting.

FORGIVENESS IS ABOUT YOU

Forgiveness is all about you. It is about you taking control of your present and future life. When Ali decided that she was not going to allow her life to be controlled by her pain and misery, she regained her life. When Ali took her pain and made it into a positive action, she started the road to self recovery.

When she was being consumed by hate she said:

My life was stolen from me. I wish I could find

the bastards who raped me and tell them what they did was wrong ... show them that they ruined my life. That they deserve to burn in hell. I hope they will.

When she forgave:

Once I realized that forgiveness was for me, that I deserved not to feel the hate any longer, I started to look at ways I could take control of my life. I decided that I needed to feel safer. I made a rule for myself that I would never drink to where I was out of control. Now I will have a beer or two, but I am always aware of my surroundings. I took a self defense class at the YMCA and thought a lot about how to be aware of my surroundings. One interesting thing about the self defense class I took was learning all the ways I can protect myself way before having to fight off an attacker.

I also had a heart to heart talk with my sister. She is three years younger than me and I wanted to make sure that she didn't get into the same trouble I got into. We took the class at the Y together.

Forgiveness needs to go from a thought to a behavior. You never say what the aggressor did was OK with you, you just know, deep within yourself, that you will not let them continue to control you through your own fears. The types of forgiveness behaviors are very personal. Some find that the behavior must be grand, while others find that subtle behaviors work best for them. It will depend on your personality. Forgiveness behavior is never revenge.

FORGIVENESS BEHAVIORS THAT HAVE WORKED FOR OTHERS

The following is a list of forgiveness behaviors that others have found to work for them. It is in no particular order. Forgiveness needs to become a behavior, but that behavior is very personal.

Smaller issues such as when someone wrongs you:

• Avoid the offending person. Know that they don't warrant your attention.

- Learn to recognize this type of person so that they can be avoided sooner.
- Forgive and then forget, move on.
- Write a letter—mail it or not.
- Talk to the person who wronged you, calmly explaining that you do not allow people to treat you that way.

Bigger issues such as when someone violates you:

- Call the police and make a formal report.
- Attend a victims' group.
- Write an article that will help others.
- Talk to a loved one, sharing what you have learned.
- Help others who are less fortunate than yourself.
- Take a self defense class.
- Write a letter—mail it or not.
- Talk to the person you are focusing on and tell them that you forgive them (with or without them understanding what this means).

What can you do for you?

_____

_____

_____

_____

Your goal is to obtain *emotion closure*. This is shrink speak for bringing an end to your emotional involvement. When you are emotionally done with the individuals who hurt you, the hurt stops. You no longer have an emotional need to focus backward, freeing you to focus on you and your future. Emotional closure is emotional freedom.

The only place where success comes before work is in the dictionary.

Vidal Sasoon
Quoting one of his teachers

SUPERFLUITY

REID:

I once asked my dad (an attorney) how he found the motivation to work through roughly 10 years of college. His answer was simple: with a mere 10 years of hard work, he earned a piece of paper that allowed him to increase his lifetime earnings fivefold. Looking at it that way, ten years doesn't seem like such a huge investment after all. I guess the tough part is looking that far into the future and convincing yourself that the effort you put forth now is worth it because it will repay you later.

HOLLY:

I was free once I learned this Life Law. "Emotional Closure" is what it is called and I find myself constantly telling people about this. If I lose anything that I have ever learned in my whole life, this is one thing that will never be lost through my journey. It is powerful stuff.

As you can see throughout this book, I have been screwed over a couple of times in my life. Being nineteen years old, one would think that I would have committed suicide by now, but because of this one life law, I was set free from my depression and all of the other strains that burdened me.

As Dr. Phil lists them, there are many ways to let out and let go of troubles, as when someone violates or wrongs you. I found my outlet in writing. After the fiasco with my stepfather I felt like I couldn't write, so all of the feelings just stewed inside of my guts, until it came to the surface so raw that when I did write I would put all of my power and energy into it, and feel so much better afterwards. Eventually, I did bring an end to my emotional involvement, the involvement that I thought I was going to carry around with me forever. Look at me now; I am putting my life out there for you to read and for you to realize that you are not the only one. This is major, you need to find an outlet, if it is music, or writing, or meditation. I strongly believe in time healing, but you have to take some control of this time. If you are just letting all of it stew, doing drugs, or locking yourself in your room because you feel like your life was robbed, do something about it. Don't you agree that all the energy it takes to be sad and distraught can be used in other ways, and don't you think that you would feel better about yourself? I do, and I do.

I don't think that I ever forgave, like Dr. Phil talks about doing in this chapter. I think that I just let it go. I wrote and lived, and didn't let myself get so sucked into being nothing, even though I might have felt like nothing many times. I remembered all of the good things that were in my life, all of the people that I had to enjoy, all of the things that I still had to learn. When I heard that my (ex) stepfather had walked free after he had ruined my life, I was crushed. But hear me now talk about it. Two years later I can talk about it and not cry, not still feel like my life is ruined. I am living, and no one, not even that selfish son of a bitch, is going to stop me.

NO NAME
(By Holly S.)

Lost in the handfuls of hurt
I am alone,
And you,
You are just a tear of the memories
I hold
One day though I will laugh,
Chuckle at your smallness.
I am tall
All the hurt I've felt
Has made me tall and oh so alive
And you,
You are nothing, oblivion, a mere shadow on the wall.
As I walk on the clouds
I look down to the blackness that follows you
I feel sorrow at first
But then I remember all the hurt that you threw into my life
So then I walk past you
Not ever looking down again . . .

I let go. I wrote. This was my outlet, my stairway to Emotional Closure.

10. Life's Law #10

Understand
what you want

"Oh yes, I see oil in your future."

10. LIFE'S LAW #10

Understand what you want

Ben was an all-American seventeen year old. His father was a doctor and his mother was a talented party planner. Life was pretty good for Ben's family. They had a nice house, three nice cars, a vacation cottage by a lake, and good friends. Ben's mother and father were worried about Ben.

His mother summed it up this way:

> Ben is a great kid. He is never in trouble, well a little pot and talking back, but he is a good kid. He is respectful and caring. I can't believe I'm even talking to a therapist. Ben is a great kid! But, he is ... how can I say it? I'll just be blunt. Ben's lazy! That's it, lazy to the core. He always has been. He just doesn't care about making something of himself. He would watch TV 'til his eyes fell out if we let him. He is a smart kid, but he just gets by with C's. He refuses to do any homework and he still gets good grades on his tests. The boy is just lazy.

When I met with Ben I asked him what he wanted most in his world. He thought about it a moment and then his face lit up with enthusiasm.

Ben: I want a 1952 Daimler-Benz 300 SL Gull-Wing. It has to be silver with a tan leather interior. It's the best car ever made. It's a work of art and fast as hell.

Dr. Phil: How come?

Ben: It's cool. It's the greatest car on the planet. In its day it won every major race in the world. It has doors that open like wings!

Dr. Phil: So how come you want the coolest car ever made?

Ben: I want to drive it around and show it off.

Keep away from people who try to belittle your ambitions. Small people always do that, but the really great make you feel that you too, can become great.

Mark Twain

Dr. Phil:	Show it off?
Ben:	That's right, I want to tool on by school and show everyone that I have made it. That I won.
Dr. Phil:	Won?
Ben:	It probably sounds bad, egotistical and all, but if I had the 300 SL Gull-Wing, I would be the coolest kid in school. Other kids would kill to hang around me.
Dr. Phil:	Other kids would be impressed?
Ben:	Absolutely. Even if you don't know about cars you would know that this car was the greatest.
Dr. Phil:	Ben, I don't understand ... do you want the car, or do you want to be the coolest kid in school?

Long pause.

Ben:	I never thought about it ... I guess I want to be popular at school.
Dr. Phil:	What would being popular at school be like for you?
Ben:	I don't get what you're saying here. I don't even like most of the kids at my school.
Dr. Phil:	I'm not talking about you liking them, I thought you were talking about them liking you?
Ben:	I guess.
Dr. Phil:	What would it be like if the kids at school liked you?
Ben:	It would be a lot easier. We would say "hi" in the hall. We would do stuff together, I guess.
Dr. Phil:	It sounds to me what you really want the most is to have a few friends and more fun in your life.
Ben:	That's not wrong, is it?

I'm using my talk with Ben to illustrate that it is hard to really know what we want out of life. I was very impressed with Ben. He showed an amazing amount of insight about himself. The above conversation and realization tends to take six to eight therapy sessions for most young adults. When asked what we want, most of us think of "stuff" that will fix our lives, then get around to realizing the "stuff" is outside of ourselves. It is nice to have, but it doesn't truly make us feel happy or safe.

Life law #10 is about truly knowing yourself. A Chinese proverb goes, *If you don't know where you are going you are already there.* It points out the importance of knowing your destination. If Ben had spent the next twenty or thirty years of his life working towards getting to a life position where he could afford such an expensive car, he most probably would not be happy with his purchase. Once he got the car, his life would probably not change all that dramatically. People would not applaud him when he got out of his snazzy auto. And, he would have the added pressure of wondering if he was liked for himself or for his money.

Ben's life started to change over the next six months. He decided it was important to him that he had friends and that he enjoyed being around people with similar interests. Ben worked on learning how to build friendships. Ben got choosy about who he befriended. Ben started to enjoy his days at school for the first time in his life. He decided that he wanted to work with people and that he thought it might be rewarding to become either a physical therapist or an emergency room doctor. Interestingly enough, when Ben started thinking about his desire to help people, his grades went up. All of a sudden he was interested in getting into a good college and learning about how he could help people. Once Ben had a goal, he figured out how to reach his goal.

Most high achievers are persuadable rather than teachable. They tend to be open minded to new ideas, but they are very cautious from whom they take ideas.

The last time I saw Ben and his mother was at Costco. He was very excited when he told me that he was going to Mexico with a church group to help build a medical clinic. His mother told me, "My Ben is such a good boy. I used to worry about him all the time, I guess I was just being silly." Ben was buying a case of bug repellent for his upcoming trip.

Lots, if not most people, get transfixed on an object that they want. They tell themselves that they will truly be happy if they get the perfect house, perfect job, or lots of money. This is bull. Research shows that Lottery winners are no happier than the general population. If they were happy before their new found wealth, then they were happy after the windfall. But, if they were bummed before, they were found to be bummed millionaires after the money arrived. You cannot buy happiness, you can only rent it. Rented happiness is short lived and not real.

When it comes to your goals you need to be specific, but not too specific. Sounds contradictory? If your goal is to be a professional basketball player, well that sounds great ... unless you are five feet in all directions. As I stated before, you may be a great basketball announcer or a great sports writer or an accomplished athletic trainer, but you are not making it in the National Basketball Association. You are stuck with the limitations the gene pool gave you. If your world orbits around pro B-ball, you need to be there. Finding your niche is what is important.

EARN

It is OK to want and to dream and to pray as long as you take your thoughts and turn them into action. In life you earn your way. Whatever your goal is you cannot simply *take* it. It is not given to you, you can't luck into it, you must earn it. The ten Life's Laws give you the foundation it takes to earn your goals. Once you have defined what you want, build your plans and make it happen. You have a limited amount of time on this planet, don't waste it—not even a little. Enjoy being you to the fullest. As I have said a few times already, *process counts*. Make the process of your life count! Do well, make yourself proud.

SUPERFLUITY

REID:

For a long time I dreamed of owning the sleekest, fastest motorcycle on the block. I would read the latest sport bike mags with endless photos of lucky testers wheeling around on the newest and fastest two-wheeled exotica and using words like "eye-popping" or "visceral" to describe the experience. I had the exact model and color scheme I wanted picked out, knew all the stats and psychotic performance figures. After reading this chapter, I think that what I probably wanted then was to be–*seen* on a motorcycle, not necessarily to ride the thing. Maybe I was silly enough to think that my new-found "outlaw appeal" would make me new friends, or have women lined up, or some such nonsense. Well, I got my bike and discovered (fortunately) that I love to ride, and also that I was missing the point entirely when I wanted a bike to boost my image. Know what you want, indeed.

HOLLY:

"If you don't know where you are going you are already there."

I have always thought that this saying was bullshit, until I really thought about it. Life will throw you curve balls, and it is up to you how you handle them; either catch them and roll with the punch, or drop them and hide from it all. Don't you want to live life to its fullest? If you don't live life to its fullest, you may become something that you don't want to become, only to look back years down the road and regret not living them.

I did drugs. I hated everyone around me and myself. I wanted to die, and I just didn't give a rat's ass about anything. But I got through it and figured out that I didn't want the life that I was living. I tried to understand what I wanted, and though I may not under-stand completely what I want right now, I totally understand what I don't want. I don't want to be a loser, I don't want to be depressed and hating myself, I don't want to be a druggy that everyone hates being around, and I for sure don't want my life to go down the toilet because a few bad things happened to me. I want to live, I want to experience life and people, I want to be successful in whatever I choose to do, and I want to be happy. I will have all of these things. I will put my mind to it and reach all the goals that I set for myself, because I am determined, unlike how I was 2 years ago.

I don't want to sound like some expert on living life, I just want you to understand that someone else has been where you are, and I am doing wonderfully. This is just to show that these Life Laws can really work if you use them. "You have a limited amount of time on this planet, don't waste it—not even a little. Enjoy being you to the fullest." Words to live by!

11. Lessons I didn't learn in shrink school

The real beginning of the term "Freudian slip."

11. LESSONS I DIDN'T LEARN IN SHRINK SCHOOL

The following are little lessons I learned from people I have had the good fortune of meeting, reading or watching. I will spare you the stories, but it is fair to assume that I learned most of the following after screwing something up.

- Spend less than you earn.
- When your wife is close to giving birth, keep gas in the car.
- Fences make good neighbors.
- Measure twice, cut once.
- Back up your hard drive.
- No matter how much JuJitsu you know, prevention is by far the best way to deal with a fight.
- Don't loan money.
- Don't sell to "friends" on credit.
- People won't let science get in the way of their religious or political beliefs.
- Fundamentalism, by definition, is closed minded.
- Question authority, especially your own.
- Teach people to treat you nicely.
- Trust behavior over words.
- Failure teaches if you pay attention.
- Bloom where you are.
- It is usually easier to ask for forgiveness than to obtain permission.
- A walk, like chicken soup, can't hurt.
- Eat lots of veggies and fruit.
- Confide in yourself. Others will allow their own fears to get in your way.

Life is either a daring adventure or nothing.

Helen Keller

Great spirits have always encountered violent opposition from mediocre minds.

Albert Einstein

12. In Closing

Be creative ... Go do well!

"Kiss me, I may be a prince."

12. IN CLOSING

Be creative ... Go do well!

Personally, I hate getting to the end of a good book when my relationship with the characters must come to an end. The end of the book means I won't get to know anything more about the characters I have spent time learning to love or hate.

This book is not that way. The end of this book is the beginning of your next life chapter. In fact, the majority of your life is probably still ahead. I wish you all the very best.

Please indulge me for one last story. I wrote it three years ago for another book*, but I think it fitting to retell here:

Years ago my wife, Geri, suggested that we take the family to a favorite camping area from her youth. She painted a beautiful picture of secluded campgrounds dotting a reflecting lake in the Adirondack Mountains of upstate New York. She talked about how we could rent canoes and paddle to the silent woods. She spoke of her hope that, if we were lucky, we could get the campground on the small island in the middle of the picture postcard lake.

Over the next few weeks we made plans to fly to the east coast and meet up with other family members to camp at Forked Lake. Our summer vacation plans came together.

As we drove to Forked Lake from Grandmothers house, the skies were gray and threatening. The weather had been cold and rainy for many days. We talked about how we were going to have to make the best of our camping trip, no matter the weather. When we got to the state campground entrance the cloud cover opened and patches of bright blue snuck through. The first thing we did was check on the availability of the island campsite. The ranger was blunt, "It's been raining for near two weeks, take your pick." We rented the island campsite and were afloat in the canoes in record time.

The lake was choppy and the wind cold. The sun threatened to burst into full light, but for now it was just hope. Ethan and I started off in our canoe. The first ten minutes were exciting as I steered the bow of the canoe towards the island. In short order, the canoe trip to the small island became work. Ethan quickly lost his enthusiasm for the sea. He was in serious need of a nap. The wind was cold and damp. The camping equipment laden the boat.

---

*Basic Parenting 101—The Manual Your Child Should Have Been Born With, Hutzpah Press, 2000. (Available at CopitchInc.com)

The mountain storm had washed a lot of debris into the lake. Steering around the floating branches and entertaining Ethan became cumbersome. After twenty minutes of paddling we met up with a cross flow of water. The wind was bitterly moist and cold. Ethan was complaining. To my surprise, the island seemed very far away.

Between the wind and drizzle, cross current, and debris, the canoe trip took over an hour. A very long hour. Setting up camp was a chore and getting everyone warm was work. But, it all worked out. We spent a magical sunny week on "our" private island.

A few months later I was talking with a couple about their two week summer vacation. It was horrible. Many things went wrong. It tried their relationship to the breaking point. By the end of the fourth day they returned home, completely upset with each other, and filed for divorce. On the advice of their friends they sought marriage counseling.

I told them the story of Forked Lake. Then continued:

> I have thought about that canoe trip often. After the weather turned nice, we canoed the same route many times. It was a leisurely twenty minute trip.
>
> I found myself thinking about how the first canoe trip was so hard. As it happened I felt frustrated. I constantly had to redirect my canoe. Something seemed to constantly pull me away from my target.
>
> I think of my marriage and my family in a similar way. I know where I want to be say, in fifty years. But, something is constantly pulling or pushing me away from that goal. On the rainy canoe trip my goal was the island. When something misdirected me, I had to navigate around it. I found a way to deal with it, as best I could, then pointed my canoe back at my target.
>
> It seems to me, that in life we are constantly blown off course and have to deal with the problem and then get ourselves back on target.

So, in closing, I hope that you hear that the process of raising yourself counts. The end result is your target island, your goal, your dream. But, the day to day process of getting to your island is the hard built foundation that is your life.

Allow yourself the peace of mind to know that you will be blown off course. And, the serenity that comes from knowing that you will deal with the problem and redirect yourself toward your island. The process counts.

Thank you for taking your time to read my book. I hope you have found it helpful.

Thank you for encouraging my behavior,

Index

Dr. Phil makes psychology usable!

Buy a book for a friend...

Basic Parenting 101
The Manual Your Child
Should Have Been Born
With

Life's Laws
For New Adults
Mastering Your Social I.Q.

www.ingramcontent.com/pod-product-compliance
Lightning Source LLC
Chambersburg PA
CBHW070139290526
45789CB00002B/552